Lineside Buildings

Nigel Digby

Ian Allan
PUBLISHING

First published 2012

ISBN 978 0 7110 3493 8

Published by Ian Allan Publishing
an imprint of Ian Allan Publishing, Ltd, Hersham, Surrey KT12 4RG.
Printed in England

Visit the Ian Allan Publishing website at www.ianallanpublishing.com

Distributed in the United States of America and Canada by BookMasters Distribution Services.

CONTENTS

Front cover *An inspiration for thousands of modellers, John H. Ahern's Madder Valley Railway."* Tony Wright, courtesy British Railway Modelling

Title page *British Railways Standard Class 3 2-6-2T No 82000 passing through Harlech station with a freight train on 11 July 1962. This scene is almost a blueprint for what we are trying to achieve as modellers.* J. Scrace, Ian Allan Library

Opposite page *The seminal scenic model railway, the Madder Valley by John Ahern, now preserved at Pendon Museum.* Tony Wright, courtesy British Railway Modelling

Introduction

Below: An
engineering train
behind Class 45 No
45072 sits on Tower
Viaduct in Bolton on
a bright Sunday in
March 1985. The
blend of terraced
housing and viaduct
is a classic model
railway scenic
opportunity.
T. Heavyside,
Ian Allan Library

A gentleman resident of East Walsham, if taking an after-breakfast stroll along the Bacton high road on a July morning in 1878, would have found unwonted activity. Where formerly a marshy field had lain fallow on the same side of the road as the canal basin, a gang of roughly attired workmen were raising fenceposts on each side of a wide strip of trampled earth, already sweating in the heat. On enquiring of the foreman, the gentleman would be told that the men were employed by a Mr Jarvis, and were building the railway line to Stalham and Great Yarmouth. Already piles of rails and sleepers had been stacked on the fenced land. The gentleman would resume his walk, remembering some of the Parliamentary activity that had gone on several years before, and feeling faintly resentful that the familiar landscape of his town would be irrevocably changed.

Of course the gentleman and his town are imaginary, but they reproduce a scene which occurred the length and breadth of the United Kingdom during most of the 19th century and some of the 20th. To imagine what it was like to construct such a railway, and to understand the reasons behind its structures is for me a vital stage in the planning of a model, where the railway is grounded in history and is properly related to the landscape it inhabits. It is easy to simply impose a model on a baseboard with no thought for its history or the country through which it runs.

Right: On 18 May
1968 Stanier '8F'
2-8-0 No 48519
banks a coal train
across Lydgate
Viaduct, Todmorden.
This scene with its
millstone grit, old
chimneys and
houses clinging to
the steep slopes
could not be
anywhere else but
the industrial valleys
of Lancashire.
Ian Allan Library

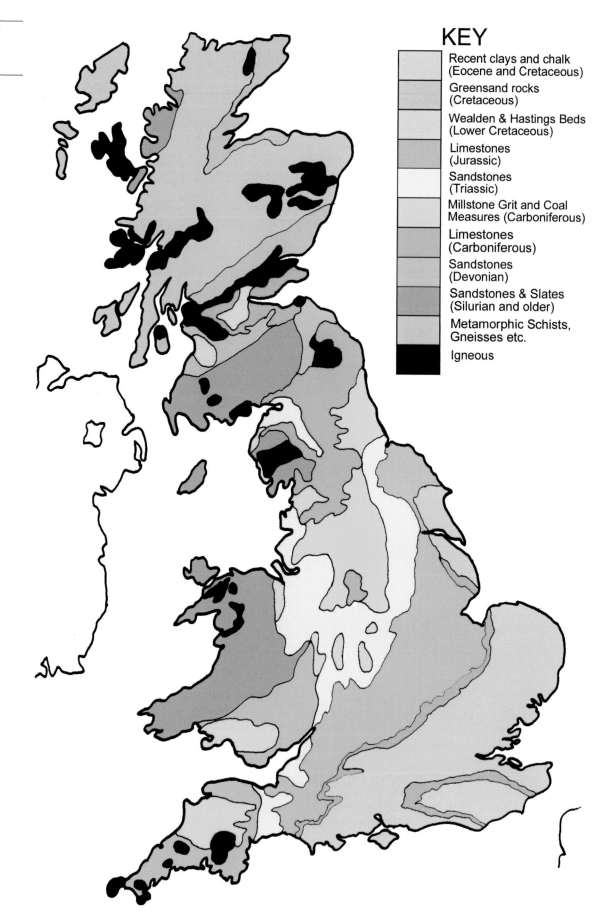

Right: Simplified geological map of Great Britain.

KEY

Recent clays and chalk (Eocene and Cretaceous)

Greensand rocks (Cretaceous)

Wealden & Hastings Beds (Lower Cretaceous)

Limestones (Jurassic)

Sandstones (Triassic)

Millstone Grit and Coal Measures (Carboniferous)

Limestones (Carboniferous)

Sandstones (Devonian)

Sandstones & Slates (Silurian and older)

Metamorphic Schists, Gneisses etc.

Igneous

My contention is that such a scheme is unrealistic, and ultimately unsatisfying. I cannot claim any originality for this idea, as several famous modellers have been mentioning it since the 1950s, but as the advice seems to pass many people by, I feel it is worth reiterating.

Regional Character

The presence of a railway altered the growth and appearance of the town or village through which it ran. Prior to the building of a line, there had been few geometric boundaries, excepting important roads and rivers or canals. Settlements tended to grow in an 'organic' way around centres, with little or no planning, using local materials. The imposition of the railway line across the landscape changed this in two ways. Firstly, the attentions of speculative builders keen to profit on the presence of the railway and the people willing to use it and live near it encouraged the construction of whole new areas of dwellings. Secondly, the straightness of the permanent way encouraged the new construction to be an orderly plan of similar houses arranged in lines following the railway, built from mass-produced and standardised components, often at variance with the local materials. The railway buildings themselves, apart from the earlier phases when railway builders were more sensitive to local requirements, could also be at variance with the local vernacular.

Great Britain is geologically very diverse, and in the 19th century the character of its local buildings reflected the availability of materials much more than it does today. When viewed overall, our island has its oldest geological deposits to the west and the north, and its newer ones to the south and the east. To the west of a line drawn roughly between the Isle of Purbeck and The Wash is the start of the more upland region of Britain, where many buildings and boundary walls were constructed from the local stone, reflecting the character of the area, and so the underlying rock must inform your choice when creating the built environment for your railway.

The most easterly of the upland stones is a relatively narrow region often referred to as the 'limestone belt', which provides us with some of our best-loved landscapes, from the Cotswolds to the North Yorkshire Moors. Beyond the limestone belt, much of the rest of Great Britain consists of sandstone, increasing in age as one travels west and north. The oldest sandstones form the Cambrian Mountains of Wales, parts of the Lake District and the Southern Uplands of Scotland. Within the sandstone are areas of other rocks, such as the millstone grit that forms the southern part of the Pennines, and the carboniferous limestone that completes the northern part of that range, and in an isolated spot to the south forms the lovely White Peak of Derbyshire.

Limestones are generally perceived as being a pale grey, which many are, but the colour varies considerably. The limestones from which the towns of Stamford and Bath are built are a warm honey shade, and much darker colours are also found. Sandstone, although it can be found in 'white' forms, does tend to be more strongly coloured, and terms such as 'New Red Sandstone' and 'Old Red Sandstone' are self-explanatory – the latter can be extremely dark red. Millstone grit is tough sandstone with large grains of quartz and is usually grey or buff, weathering to black. Indeed, owing to the universal use of coal, black deposits of soot would have masked many of the differences between stones in our towns and cities until revealed by recent cleaning.

Volcanic activity has also played its part in providing the materials of Britain, both directly in the way of granites and basalts, and indirectly in the metamorphosing of other rocks exposed to the heat and pressure. Because of their resistance to weathering, these igneous rocks tend to form uplands, such as Dartmoor, Snowdonia, the Cumbrian Mountains of the Lake District and the Cheviot Hills of the Borders. Most of the Scottish Highlands are formed of igneous and metamorphic rocks. In Wales, Cornwall and Cumbria, the proximity to the volcanic activity metamorphosed some of the older sedimentary stones into slate.

To the east of our imaginary line, the newest deposits are clays and alluvial soils overlaying a basin of chalk deposited in the Cretaceous period. The chalk

Above: *An example
of the classical style,
Monkwearmouth in
Sunderland, built in
1848 by Thomas
Moore. Now out of
railway use, it has
found new life as a
museum. I. S. Carr,
Ian Allan Library*

landscape of rolling downs and dry valleys is an attractive one, but does not yield
much in the way of building stone, although certain varieties of hard chalkstone
were employed. The most useful stones were actually from a series of beds
exposed beside the chalk, known as the 'Greensand'. These were sandstones,
often coloured by iron oxide into a range from greenish yellow to chocolate brown.
They were of only local significance with names such as 'Reigate stone', or in
Norfolk 'Carstone'. A limestone also associated with the Greensand was the
'Kentish Rag', a tough, brittle stone once much used in London. Some sandstone
was also quarried from the Weald, but generally only clay, sand and shale were
found here and good stone was at such a premium in the Southeast that a tradition
of timber building was maintained, particularly using weatherboarding.

On the clays of Norfolk, Suffolk and Essex, the southern parts of Dorset and
Hampshire and north Kent, when stone was required for special buildings such as
churches, it was imported. For ordinary buildings, timber framing or earth 'Cob'
walls were the traditional materials until the rise in popularity of brickwork in the
17th and 18th centuries. Many local brickyards were founded in these clay-rich
areas to supply local building needs. Flint, picked up from the fields or from the
beach, and knapped (split) or used as pebbles, supplemented the brick, which was
used for quoins and lintels.

The rise in the use of brick during the great Victorian expansion of our cities
and industrial areas meant that in places where hitherto brick had been a rarity, it

Right: *Built in 1838,
the classical Curzon
Street terminus of
the London &
Birmingham Railway
was designed by
Philip Hardwick as
an Ionic companion
piece to the Doric
propylaeum at
Euston. For most
of its life it was used
as a Goods Office,
and has now been
restored.
Ian Allan Library*

Above: The Jacobean style as used at Louth in 1848. After closure to passengers in 1970, the building decayed as seen in this 1977 view, and would have been demolished had it not been Listed Grade II. It has now been restored and converted into flats. S. Creer, Ian Allan Library

now began to supplant the indigenous materials, often with poor effects for the fabric of the settlement. By the end of the 19th century, brick had spread from the east to almost all parts of England and Wales, although it remained rare in Cornwall, the Cotswolds and the Lake District. Scotland escaped its imposition until more recent times.

The colour of a brick depends very much on the clay it is made from, and some clays, such as those in the Midlands and the North give bright reds, an unfortunate clash of colour if the predominant masonry in a town or villages is the local stone. Fortunately, the range of colours was usually of softer tones, such as the 'white' (actually yellow-white) bricks common around Peterborough, Cambridge and the Fens, the 'grey' (actually light brown) of the London stock brick, and the soft yellows, oranges and pinks of Norfolk and Suffolk. Later in the 19th century, railways and other civil engineering projects needed tougher bricks, and strong, impermeable engineering bricks were developed in Staffordshire, in blue and orange-red colours. The blue features particularly on railways, for bridge construction and retaining walls, although rarely for station buildings.

Thus it can be seen that the decline in local techniques in the 20th century is mainly due to the railways themselves, enabling the distribution of machine-made bricks, Welsh slate and Portland cement countrywide, and encouraging a uniformity that would have been unknown hitherto.

A Hierarchy of Structures

There are numerous ways of setting your model in place and time. The most obvious ones are the locomotives and rolling stock, followed closely by the signalling. However, the buildings and structures have their own tales to tell, too, not only about the owning company but also when and how the line was built, and what status it was. By taking some general points, one can make a checklist of features that will help in the construction of a realistic model, or in understanding the features of a location that the modeller wishes to reproduce in miniature.

The first factor to establish is the time period in which the railway was built. By disregarding the first, mineral-only railways, and by considering that almost all significant railway construction was finished by the First World War, the time periods are perhaps threefold: early (1830–1844), expansion (1845–1870) and consolidation (1871–1914).

The early period saw the establishment of most of the trunk routes, which are still with us today, with the occasional branch line. It was also the time of the famous engineers and architects. Their response to the process of railway building can be summarised in one word: bold.

The route of a railway is a careful choice between direction, availability of land, and terrain. It is well understood by anyone with an interest in railway construction that there was more than one way to build between two points. The original method used to a great extent by the Stephensons and Brunel was to build the most level route possible, so that the steam locomotives of the time could cope. If this required a roundabout route, or long tunnels, then so be it. The other main school of thought was to follow the method of the Stephensons' pupil and later rival Joseph Locke. This reduced the civil engineering works by allowing steeper gradients, as Locke was convinced that locomotives would soon be more powerful, which they were.

Below: Faultless merging of railway and buildings on the EM gauge Kingstorre by Robert Dudley-Cooke. Tony Wright, courtesy British Railway Modelling

The same boldness was true of the architecture of the lines concerned. These great trunk routes had the benefit of gifted engineers who could design a consistent series of buildings, or could employ the top architects of the day. Their aim was to impress the public with monumental designs, such as the Doric entrance to Euston station, and reassure them with the comforting familiarity of classical or 'Tudor'-style station buildings.

Thus the overall impression of this early phase is of innovative engineering involving immense viaducts, long tunnels, deep cuttings and high embankments. The buildings were of a high standard, many of them with architectural merit, and a consistent character, responsive to local materials and styles.

The middle, expansion period was the time when most of the rest of the network was completed, with some trunk lines (eg, the Great Northern Railway), and a maze of secondary lines and branches. The first decade included the 'Railway Mania' and the inevitable slump, followed by years of cut-throat competition. Money was not quite as readily found, and a number of small companies were very poor indeed. But it was also the era of the formation of the great railway companies from earlier constituents such as the Midland, the London & North Western and the Great Eastern.

The larger and more important railways could afford to employ the great engineers of their day. These lines still featured many impressive and iconic

Below: The Italianate style as practised by Brunel, seen here at Theale (1847) in 1963. The round-headed windows and oversailing roof are very distinctive. This station has been demolished, but fortunately the similar Mortimer has survived. M. Hale, Ian Allan Library

Above: Great Northern Railway Italianate at Welwyn North. This station was built in 1850 by the famous contractor Thomas Brassey, and until 1926 was known simply as Welwyn. The building is now Listed Grade II. D. Percival, Ian Allan Library

engineering works. At the other end of the spectrum were the lines with very little capital, many of them promoted during the Mania years. Large works would be avoided if at all possible, there being a trade-off between capital costs and working expenses. A railway built with a ruling gradient of 1 in 100 would cost less to build than one with 1 in 300, but would be more expensive to operate.

Architecturally, this was the time of Victorian eclecticism, a mixed bag of almost any style applied randomly from line to line. Gothic, Tudor, Jacobean, Cottage Orné, Classical, French Renaissance and Italianate all rubbed shoulders. The period can be summed up by the juxtaposition of two of London's termini: the austere King's Cross (1850), and the exuberant St Pancras (1867). Poorer companies, however, had to make do with more mundane buildings, at their worst little more than wooden sheds.

The final period saw fewer lines built, and the emergence of a standardised approach under a company engineer. Design of railways was brought 'in-house', and a universal method emerged combining the best of the Stephenson and Locke ideas. The Settle & Carlisle line of the Midland Railway, opened at the beginning of the period, and the Great Central Railway London Extension opened at the end are perhaps the best exemplars of this.

Station buildings also reflected the move towards standardisation. During the 1880s many railways evolved a typical style by which they could be identified, and as stations were expanded or rebuilt, this was what they used. The plethora of architectural styles fell out of fashion. A more detailed overview of station architecture will be given in the appropriate chapter.

As well as the superb main-line work, this period was the heyday of the 'contractor's line'. From the experiences of the early days, it became obvious that railway building was a specialist skill requiring a specialist contractor. Names such as Thomas Brassey became synonymous with good contracting, followed by many lesser imitators. From their offices, usually to be found on Victoria Street, Westminster, these contractors and engineers obtained contracts from all around the world. However, when the work was in danger of drying up, gaps in the existing national railway system were sought, and lines actively promoted in order to keep the firms going. These were the 'contractor's lines'. A local peer or other wealthy landowner was used as a figurehead, and some of the more influential local people were recruited onto the Boards of these little companies in order to give credibility, but the usual result after a few years was to sell out to one of the larger railway companies. It is not generally realised that a high mileage of the national system, in particular the secondary lines and branches, was built in this way, most of which fell prey to the closures of the late 1950s and 60s.

Many of the contractor's lines were extremely light on works, being laid almost directly on the ground, with just enough earthworks to prevent (where possible) gradients exceeding a maximum of 1 in 100. Bridges, where present, were modest, and level crossings were tolerated, sometimes in great numbers.

Below: William Tress, a pupil of Sir William Tite, designed a number of stations for the South Eastern Railway. Robertsbridge is an example of his Italianate style from 1852, seen here in 1986. J. Scrace, Ian Allan Library

Above: The typical 'Kentish Clapboard' of the South Eastern Railway at Pluckley (1842) in 1982. This type of timberwork is more properly known as weatherboarding. L. Bertram, Ian Allan Library

Scope of the Book

The philosophy behind this book is twofold. Firstly, I will be broadly covering the type of buildings you may actually need for your layout, and their history, function and the differences between them. Secondly, I will be focusing on some case studies, where there will be some examples of model construction where appropriate. This is not so much to show you exactly how to build lineside structures, but just the way that I do them, from which you may be able to take some hints on how to make your own. The book will not be a detailed treatise on how to build every structure under the sun, or how to cope with layers of plastic sheet, nor will it show you how to build the legions of available kits, a subject that has already been covered extensively by other authors.

I will be citing examples of stations, goods sheds and other railway buildings from all over Great Britain, although my core research has always been on the Midland & Great Northern Joint Railway, which I know intimately. Inevitably, therefore, most case studies in this book will be based on the structures of that line, but of course its practices were similar to railways up and down the country. What I have done is to select photographs to illustrate these practices, hopefully to inspire and assist the modeller with their own structures.

CHAPTER

Materials, Method and Research

When you want to employ a builder to erect a house or an extension, you of course need drawn plans. Modelling is just the same; it's no good thinking you can make it up as you go along. A set of drawings, however simple, is essential. For a model of a particular building or structure you may be lucky and find a drawing already available. This may be in a book or a magazine, and it's always worth looking through old railway modelling magazines. Failing this, you may venture to the National Railway Museum, the National Archives, or to the individual line societies.

If no drawing is forthcoming, then you will have to do it yourself. To begin collecting information about the buildings or bridges you wish to construct, naturally you start from the ground and work up. Maps are a vital source – the larger the scale the better. The Ordnance Survey 1:2500 scale maps of various dates are of course ubiquitous. If you can obtain a 1:500 plan of your station or other location by the railway company itself, this is usually extremely reliable.

Photographs are another essential. The vast majority of railway photographs are from the 1950s and 60s. Fortunately, if you model an earlier period, change inside the railway fence was not particularly rapid, and the chances are that your building probably looked very much the same 50 years before. Photographs from the present day, if your building still exists, are useful too, as they can show the colours of materials used, and even if they have been altered in modern times it is often easy to see the recent additions, especially when read in conjunction with the 1:2500 maps. Aerial photographs, either from books, Blom Aerofilms, or the National Monuments Record are an invaluable tool, and they may fill in gaps about obscure corners of your site that had escaped ordinary photography altogether.

Having got an outline of the floor plan, and deduced changes to it that may have occurred before or after your historical period, the next step is to measure the building itself. First, you must obtain permission from the owner/occupier. In my experience, once you explain just what it is you are doing, owners are usually quite happy for you to take measurements and notes, so long as you are quick about it. Make sure you have a clipboard and plenty of paper, a good *long* measuring tape (30 metres/100 feet is recommended), pens, pencils, and a good camera.

Take photographs and make a sketch of each part of the building or bridge you are measuring. By far the quickest and most accurate way of measuring is to take 'running' dimensions; you start from one zero point and pick up measurements of doors, windows, pipes, etc as you go along the tape, writing them on the sketch. Heights can be recorded in a similar way, but it is often quicker to count brick or stone courses, provided you measure enough of them to get an average height first; I usually measure 10 courses.

You may be unlucky, and find that what you want to model has been swept away by new development, or alternatively you are building something that didn't actually exist. In these cases, see if you can find and measure a similar building, or use one from the same line or company. An inappropriate building will detract from the sense of place and time you are trying to build up on your model. On my layout 'East Walsham', a fictional location, I am using railway buildings culled from nearby M&GN stations such as Stalham, and choosing prototypes from the town and the countryside around it for buildings outside the fence.

The last resort is to work entirely from photographs. This is not as difficult as it may sound. You can still count brick courses, and plan dimensions can be estimated from the 1:2500 maps. With the advent of photographic manipulation programs on the computer, even an oblique view can be treated to remove perspective and expanded to the correct proportions.

Right: Stamford Town, designed by Sancton Wood and built in the local honey-coloured limestone in 1848. This was a conscious attempt by the Syston & Peterborough Railway, a satellite of the Midland Railway, to match the station to the town.
G. Mann,
Ian Allan Library

Tools and Equipment

After your researches, you need to draw up your elevations to the scale of your model. I would recommend you obtain a drawing board; a small A3 size board with simple parallel motion is amply sufficient, and an adjustable set square. Drawing pens are not really needed, as you will probably do most of your work in pencil. A good propelling pencil with 0.35mm or 0.5mm diameter leads of HB or 2H grade is better than a conventional pencil for even line and tone. A steel rule is required for marking off measurements in millimetres. You will also need compasses, dividers and of course masking tape to secure your paper.

Tools for model building are usually light. A selection of needle files of round, square, triangular and flat sections have a multitude of uses. Some small long-nosed pliers are essential for holding or picking up small items. Wire cutters can be used for nibbling away at Plastikard, wood and card as well as cutting lengths of thin wire. A scriber is needed to make brick and stone courses in sheet materials, or to encourage them to bend; I use an old compass from a schoolboy drawing set I had long ago. A pin chuck, when holding an old-fashioned gramophone needle, makes a good scriber too, and also holds very small diameter drills, suitable for defining the corners of windows and doors and numerous other tasks where even a hand drill would be too rough.

For cutting, I prefer a scalpel. I find the Stanley knife too large for fine work, and the disposable so-called craft knives are too coarse for my taste. I use size 10A or 11 blades in my scalpel. An A3 size cutting board of the self-sealing type gives the best surface to cut on. A large mirror or piece of glass ensures a dead flat surface on which to assemble your walls when they are cut out.

Below: A page of site notes by the author, meant to be read in conjunction with photographs taken on the day.

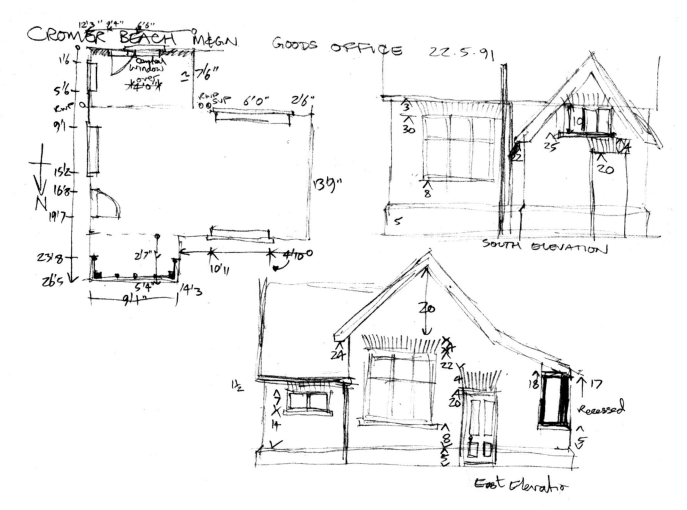

Surfaces sometimes need to be smoothed or shaped, and for this some glasspaper of medium and fine grades is handy, particularly if you are working with wood. For finer work, the grey 'wet and dry' type of paper is indispensable.

For painting I use a variety of brushes, from very small to large sizes, flat and round section, and I always use the best I can afford. The types marketed for use with acrylic paints, sold in roll-up sets, I find particularly suitable. Cheap brushes shed their bristles on your nice new paint.

Heavier tools I use frequently are a portable vice, hand-held screwdrivers, a small wood plane, a hand drill and a pin hammer. Saws are sometimes needed, and I have several from rip saws down to a junior hacksaw. Power tools are indispensable for making baseboards, as is a small variable-speed multi-tool, which can be used for drilling, sanding, buffing and so on.

A small soldering iron and stand comes in very handy. It's surprising how many items can be made up from soldered wire and tube. A clip-on heat sink prevents the unwanted effects of too much heat, and being sprung, can be used to hold items that need to be glued into position without pressure from the hand.

Above: The imposing exterior of Windsor & Eton (Riverside) in 1977. The architect Sir William Tite, conscious that Queen Victoria would be using the station regularly, designed a flamboyant Tudor composition, opened by the London & South Western Railway in 1848. J. G. Glover, Ian Allan Library

Materials

For me, the most versatile material for the construction of buildings and bridges is simply card. The usual card I use is sold as 'mounting board', and is 1.5mm thick, with a variety of colours on one side only. For a while I was able to get a much better card from a local picture framer, which was called 'illustration board'. This was a much firmer card, although a similar thickness, with no tendency to separate into layers as mounting board can when mistreated. There are rough and smooth surface finishes available, but it is a more specialist product and not so readily available as mounting board.

For thicker construction, a material sold as 'foamcore board' is very useful, being a foam interior sandwiched between two layers of thin card. The foam does not respond well to spirit-based adhesives, however, so care has to be taken when jointing. Available thicknesses are 3mm, 5mm and 10mm.

For thicker construction where rigidity is absolutely essential, for example buildings in scales such as 10mm/foot, plywood is the normal resource. Try to get European birch plywood, which is consistent in quality. There is a range of thicknesses, but 3mm (1/8 inch) or 6mm (1/4 inch) are probably the most common. Plywood does need more work than foamcore board, and cutting out window and door positions can be a laborious task. A modern equivalent and substitute for plywood is MDF, again in a variety of thicknesses. It has the advantage of having no grain, unlike plywood, but can be labour-intensive to work. The other commonly

Above: *One of Sir
William Tite's more
modest stations
for the LSWR's
Barnstaple line,
King's Nympton,
opened in 1854.
Tudor in flavour, it
is built of local stone,
randomly coursed.
Its original name until
1951 was South
Molton Road.*
Ian Allan Library

Above: *Common
types of brick bonding;
from left to right –
Flemish, English and
stretcher bond.*

used board, chipboard, is really only suitable as a baseboard on which your buildings can be assembled.

At the other end of the spectrum, thinner card and cartridge paper are very useful for shapes that thicker card cannot attain, or for thin panelling on walls or doors. The usefulness of plain Plastikard, of 10 thousandth to 60 thousandth of an inch thickness (0.25mm to 1.5mm), and a variety of colours, is too well known for me to be able to add anything here.

For windows, clear Plastikard can be obtained, but alternatives are Perspex and polycarbonate sheet, both of which are more difficult to work but, unlike Plastikard, are rigid. Some workers have used thin glass of the type sold for microscope slides, but I have no experience of this material.

Absolutely indispensable for the modelling of chimney pots, water pipes, roof columns and the other miscellaneous items present on buildings are the small sections in wood, metal and plastic now available in model shops under various

Right: The Plastikard
moulds and some
rejected examples
of bridge caps.

brand names. Wood in the form of obechi, spruce or balsa can come in square, rectangular and round sections of various sizes, all about 450 to 600mm in length. Metal in the form of brass, copper and aluminium can be found in rods, tubes and rectangular or square box sections. Plastic has a similar range, with the addition of H, L and I sections, good for representing rolled joists. Sizes again vary, but lengths tend to be shorter at around 300mm.

For the representation of the material in which the building was constructed, it is usual to apply printed brick and stone papers, embossed card and paper, or embossed Plastikard of the correct type. It is wise to be aware of the different types of coursing. Until the 1920s, brickwork for buildings was almost universally in solid walls of 'Flemish bond'. In the 1920s and 30s cavity walls made their appearance, for which 'stretcher bond' was used, although until the 1950s it was often disguised with rendering or half-timbering. Bridges, other engineering works and a great many railway buildings used 'English bond'. Stonework could be 'ashlar' with each stone cut and smoothed into the same size and laid strictly in courses; 'coursed rubble' where stones of different sizes are dressed squarely and laid in strict or varying courses; and 'random rubble' in which stones of widely varying size are laid undressed and in no particular coursing.

Timber could be erected in a number of ways too. Horizontal boarding came in two types: weatherboarding and lapped boarding. Each board above overlaps the top of the board below, but in weatherboarding there is little or no rebating of the boards, so each one presents an angled face. Lapped boarding is more

Below: Measured
drawing of a plate
girder bridge.

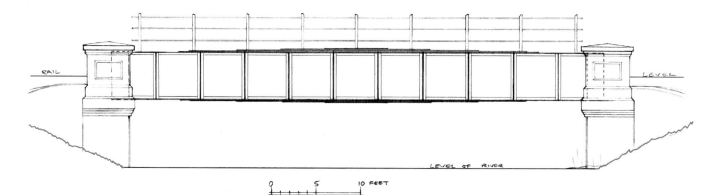

sophisticated, there being rebates at top and bottom of each board so that they lie flush to the side of the building. Vertical boarding or matchboarding was popular with some companies, such as the Great Northern. This boarding was laid flush, usually tongue-and-groove. The vertical joints were often emphasised with v-joints, and some were battened; that is, covered with small square battens. Occasionally, boarding of this kind would be laid diagonally.

The value of modelling clays such as Das cannot be overstated. They can be laid over the wall surface and pressed or carved into the desired coursing if none is available in embossed form. They can also be moulded or carved into the odd shapes that are sometimes required for dressed stone, plus a myriad of other uses. Ordinary domestic fillers like Polyfilla should not be overlooked either. I find this useful for casting into a number of identical items, such as caps for bridge pillars.

The number of adhesives required is many and varied. My usual method of joining card is an impact adhesive such as Evo-Stik, but other glues such as UHU and Bostik are also needed, principally because they give you time to position the object being glued. White woodworking glue like Resin W is essential for wood joints, or just gluing paper. Liquid styrene solvent, brushed into the joints, has largely superseded polystyrene glue in a tube for joining plastics, although it would be as well to have both. To strengthen glued joints in ply or other woods, a choice from a variety of small brass and steel panel pins and nails is also desirable.

Above A '1959 Stock' train leaving Blake Hall for Epping in 1977. Originally built for the Great Eastern Railway, Blake Hall is an example of its so-called '1865 style'. Electrified by London Underground in 1957, the station was closed in 1981 and is now a private residence. J. G. Glover, Ian Allan Library

The traditional method of colouring the finished building is to use enamel paints from small tins, such as Humbrol, and modellers usually build up a collection of a large number of these over the years. Acrylic paints are now just as popular, and there is no reason why other paint types cannot be pressed into service, including household paint and car spray paint. The grey primer of this type can be particularly useful. Needless to say, gloss paint should be outlawed from your buildings; eggshell or matt are the order of the day. I have also used coloured pencils and pastel sticks to good effect. A black pastel stick is a quick way to add sooty weathering to embossed brickwork.

Building Methods

Once all the research is over the drawings need to be done. They are not only a record of the building itself but also your working drawings for the entire project. Quite a bit of forethought is required at this stage. Do you use simple butt joints at the corners? Are you putting interior details? What method are you using for your windows and doors? How deep are the reveals? Is the building to be internally lit? Where does the wiring go? Does the roof need to come off? Solving all these questions now, while still on the drawing board, can save a world of pain later.

After the drawings are completed, I prefer to build what I call the 'carcass' of the building. I mark out the walls and their openings on the chosen material, cut them out and assemble. This is an exciting moment, because for the first time you get an inkling of what your building will be like, its bulk and appearance from unusual angles.

Below: Midland standardisation 1. The instantly recognisable outline of a Settle & Carlisle station, seen here at Appleby. Opened in 1870, this station was built of brick, although most others on the line were local stone. The name was changed to Appleby West in 1948, reverting to Appleby in 1962. British Railways, Ian Allan Library

Other basic structural items can be made now, such as internal walls, roofs and chimneys. If no internal walls are proposed, there will still need to be interior bracing to prevent movement. If the building requires an unobstructed interior, such as a goods shed, then make sure the carcass is built of a rigid material that will not move or warp over time. The aim is to create the basic form of the building, but as a shell without fittings and finishes. Items such as the roof can remain unattached so as to leave the walls unobstructed and to make it easier to apply tiles or slates.

Next comes the cladding. It may sometimes be expedient to clad the carcass when it is still unassembled, particularly if you are using a Plastikard brick or stone cladding, which takes more work than a printed or embossed paper covering. The area of most difficulty in Plastikard is the corner. I have seen several good models spoiled by the corner brick courses not matching up, the result of slight misalignment when gluing on prior to assembly. In addition, butt joints are unacceptable, except perhaps for window reveals, and the corner edges of the plastic sheet must be chamfered to make an invisible joint. Further complication is introduced, especially in the more visible larger scales, when the arrangement of the brickwork at a corner in Flemish bond or English bond is considered. A brick cut to half its width, called a 'queen closer' has to be introduced to maintain the

Above Midland standardisation 2. The ridge-and-furrow platform canopy was fitted to many Midland stations, and developed from Paxton's design for the Crystal Palace. Although under threat in the 1970s, the canopy was saved and has since been restored. C. J. Tuffs, Ian Allan Library

brick spacing. Some sheets incorporate corners of this kind into their manufacture, so you can have the correct appearance. For window and door reveals, it is acceptable to butt the thin piece of brickwork to the inner face of the cladding, and notch each mortar joint with a needle file, before rubbing with 'wet and dry' paper. The joint all but disappears if done carefully. For stonework, it would probably be best to use modelling clay in these areas.

Another headache is how to make invisible joins in sheets if the wall to be covered is a large one. About the only thing to do is to make the join irregular, wandering first one way and then the other, using the mortar joints to guide your cuts and of course ensuring that both sheets are cut the same! Clay or filler can then smooth off the gaps. Where a rainwater downpipe is prominent, the opportunity can be taken to have a vertical joint hidden behind it.

Where Plastikard cladding is used on the exterior, it is advisable to add a comparable thickness of plain Plastikard to the interior, otherwise the card warps very badly. I didn't believe this myself at first, until I saw it in action. The effect with embossed card and paper is fortunately less pronounced, but a lot of internal bracing is advisable.

If the area of wall is too small to justify fiddling around with bits of plastic, or perhaps if the surface texture you need is not covered by any of the existing cladding materials, then embossing the surface of the card yourself is a solution, if rather time-consuming. This can be done with a scriber, but I prefer to use a very hard pencil, 4H or harder, so I can see where I've been.

When the cladding has been added, doors and windows can be inserted in their apertures. I prefer to paint the walls, both inside and out, before fixing these details. The windows and doors themselves can be made up from layers of Plastikard, or card and paper on the glazing of your choice, or from the expanding list of commercially available alternatives in brass, white metal or plastic. The moving parts of windows, be they sashes or casements, were usually painted

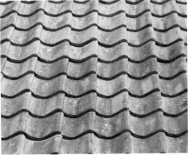

Above Common types of roofing material; from left to right – plain tile, slate and pantile.

Above Great Central Railway standardisation. The GCR London Extension was opened in 1899 and almost all stations were of the island platform type with access from road bridges, just as here at Helmdon. Passenger services were withdrawn in 1963. J. H. Russell, Ian Allan Library

white, whatever the company colour of the frames or mullions. I would advise painting them a light grey, rather than white, which always looks too glaring at small scales.

Roofs can be complicated assemblies in themselves, with bargeboards, fascia boards and guttering, as well as the slates or tiles. I use strips of thin card, or paper in smaller scales, scribed or half-cut to represent the joints between each adjacent tile and slate. Slates are usually quite large, 20" long by 10" wide being a popular size known as 'countess', and can be purplish grey (Welsh) or greenish grey (Westmorland and Cornwall). Plain tiles tend to be smaller than slates, with more pronounced joints, and of course are a red-brown colour. Pantiles, large clay tiles with a surface moulded into one, two or three ripples, are arranged in vertical

Above: W. N. Ashbee was the GER's gifted architect for several decades and designed many fine stations in the Domestic Revival style. This example is Hertford East, opened in 1888. L. Bertram, Ian Allan Library

strips without the brickwork-style alternation of plain tiles, and are a more East Anglian phenomenon.

Chimneys can be treated just the same as for the walls, but where they penetrate the roof there will be lead flashing, an item that is often forgotten. I use aluminium cooking foil, which is malleable and can be persuaded into odd shapes and corners. I cut it into strips and glue it shiny side down. The dull side can then be painted light grey. Where flashing meets brickwork or stonework, it is generally keyed into each course with a backward slope below, the result looking rather like teeth. Chimney pots can be made from metal or plastic sections or purchased as white metal castings from various manufacturers. Decorative ridge tiles can be folded up from card or again purchased as castings or even etched brass. The number of accessories available to the modeller of buildings is expanding all the time.

There are too many other details on a building to list individually here, but particularly important are rainwater goods. Gutters, which until the postwar period were usually square or ogee in section, can simply be made up from plastic or metal sections, with rod or tube as the downpipes, although once again the trade can come to the rescue with a number of cast white metal items. Of the other details, such as platform canopies or enamel signs, more is stated in the relevant sections.

Above *From the 1880s, the London Brighton & South Coast Railway rebuilt many of its older stations. At Lewes, originally opened on this site in 1857, the company rebuilt the station with a lantern over the booking hall in 1889.* L. Bertram, Ian Allan Library

Low-Relief Buildings

Up to now, I have been assuming that a building will be modelled 'in the round', that is a finished product viewable from all sides. This is not always required. To save space, a building may actually only be a frontage, with little more than one or two inches (25 – 50mm) depth. On my own 'East Walsham' layout, there is no room for anything other than low-relief terraces in the background. Low-relief buildings are transitional between the fully modelled foreground and the flat scenic background. In fact, if handled judiciously, they can make any flat painted or photographic backscene unnecessary.

All the usual methods are applied to the visible parts of the half-relief model, but of course the rear need not be finished off. In fact the opportunity should be taken to brace the structure as much as possible, as the stability usually given by the box structure of the building is lacking. If an effect of greater distance is desired, then the model itself can be at a slightly smaller scale than the rest of the layout, provided it is followed through with any figures or vehicles that stand next to it! Colours will tend to be more subdued, too.

CHAPTER

Civil Engineering

The type of bridge encountered is for our purposes determined from the perspective of the railway. Underbridges allowed roads, other railways, streams, rivers and canals to pass beneath the line, and overbridges allowed the same to pass over the line. Tunnels are essentially extended overbridges.

The civil engineering of a particular railway can be its most obvious feature, the numerous viaducts and tunnels of the Midland's Settle & Carlisle line, for example. Bridges can be divided up into classes: masonry bridges, rolled joist bridges, plate girder bridges, and lattice girder bridges. As can be seen, there is a considerable vocabulary of terms used to refer to the various types of bridges and their construction, and some of this will be explained in the relevant sections.

The materials used for civil engineering changed over time. Whereas many of the works of the earlier period were done in the local stone or brick of the area, eventually the blue engineering brick became almost universal for railway use, either as piers or abutments for steel girders, or for entirely masonry bridges and viaducts. It was not unusual to see an older red brick structure patched or partially rebuilt with blue bricks, producing an interesting parti-coloured effect. Concrete, at first hidden behind brick facings, had been present in railway structures since the middle of the 19th century, but began to make its presence felt visually from the 1890s. Reinforced or ferro-concrete is the standard civil engineering material of the present day.

Earthworks

Most lowland railways in Britain were cut through ordinary earth or 'loam'. This falls naturally into a slope of 1 in 1½, an angle of about 35 degrees, and so most cuttings and almost all embankments had this slope. Cutting through rock allowed

Below: The segmental arches and coursed rubble of Arten Gill Viaduct on the Settle & Carlisle line of the Midland exemplifies the civil engineering of the whole route as it supports Class 5MT 4-6-0 No 45112 on a southbound freight in 1966. J. Clarke, Ian Allan Library

steep sides at a slope of 8 to 1, requiring less land, but conversely wet clay or peat required slopes of 1 in 4. Through built-up areas, retaining walls or viaducts were common to restrict the width of the right of way to the minimum necessary.

Culverts

By far the most numerous class of bridge is entirely unnoticed by the traveller. Culverts allow drainage ditches or small streams to pass under a line. While visually unimportant, culverts were necessary to maintain the drainage of the land surrounding the railway.

The usual span for a culvert was three to five feet. At its simplest, a culvert needed only to be stout timber beams supported on timber piling, and this was common on low-status contractor's lines or light railways, but for longevity, masonry was always the best option. A masonry culvert would usually consist of three rings of brickwork arched over a concrete invert, sometimes with a small parapet. As an alternative, rolled joists could be used instead of a masonry arch.

Masonry Bridges

For the small-span bridge, or viaducts of multiple small spans, the first choice was usually to build an arch or arches from masonry, in stone or brick. Masonry bridges are divided into three classes: semicircular, segmental and semi-elliptical.

A masonry bridge is made up of several components, structural, practical and (in the case of railways) decorative. The essential part was of course the arch. This

Above: The elliptical eastern portal of Disley Tunnel (2m 346yds). The wyvern seen over the portal is a symbol the Midland Railway used extensively. H. Weston, Ian Allan Library

Above: *A typical*
underline culvert.

was invariably constructed on a 'centring' of timber. Stone was the choice of the early railway pioneers, remaining in favour in the stone-using districts. Elsewhere, brick was the favoured material, and came to overtake stone, so much so that many otherwise stone-built bridges had brick arches. Unlike an arch over an opening in a building, where the bricks were arranged vertically, brick arches for bridges were made up of 'rings' of brickwork, laid horizontally on their small side. Being independent of each other, the rings were able to cope with the geometry of the arch without excessive mortar gaps between each brick. A typical number of arch rings for a masonry bridge was five.

A brick arch is also the ideal medium for coping with a 'skew' bridge, where the crossing of the railway is at an angle. The major way of dealing with this in Great Britain was the English or 'helicoidal' method, developed in the late 18th and early 19th centuries. In these cases, only the line of bricks at top centre of each arch is at right angles to the main face of the bridge. The effect inside the arch, the intrados or soffit, is of a spiral of brick courses, ending at a calculated angle on the abutment, the outer ends of the bricks in each ring presenting a more angular aspect the further away from the centre of the arch they are. There are more ways to create a skew arch but, as they are more complex to build, did not become as popular among engineers as the English method.

The abutments, the vertical walls rising from foundation level on each side of the span, meet the thrust of the arch. On a viaduct, the arches between the abutments are supported upon towers of masonry known as piers, their height adjusted according to the terrain the railway is crossing. Sometimes it happens that a viaduct has to be curved, and in this situation the piers are built to be wider on the outside of the curve, allowing the arches to remain a uniform size. For a skew bridge, the piers would assume the form of a parallelogram.

Between the curve of the arch and the abutments is an area of plain brickwork forming the spandrel, a name shared with the cast iron items often found supporting platform canopies. Above the crown of the arch and the spandrels was the deck, kept level to carry railway formations, but often curved into a shallow arch for roadways. Drainage pipes were embedded into the concrete infilling to carry away harmful water. On each side were built the parapet walls, often quite high on public road overbridges, but relatively low on railway underbridges, later supplemented with safety rails for the protection of permanent way staff. The parapet walls were capped to keep them water-resistant, usually with special rounded 'bull-nose' engineering bricks.

At each end the parapet walls were thickened into pillars, topped off with caps. Sometimes the caps were genuine stone, but more often than not, especially in the lowland districts, they were 'artificial stone', a concrete incorporating powdered stone as its aggregate. This versatile material was used for many 'stone' details on bridges and buildings during the railway era.

Between the parapet and the structural part of the bridge was the string course,

Below: *A semicircular arch cattle creep.*

Above: *An elliptical masonry bridge, No 299 on the North Norfolk Railway.*

four or five courses of brick standing a few inches proud of the surface and topped with a sloped bevel brick to throw off rain. The parapets, pillars and string course served no engineering function, but were purely practical and decorative. In this regard, there was no reason why the parapet walls should not be as flat as the roadway or track formation, but it was the usual practice to build the brickwork up so that the top of the wall formed a subtle curve, very much in the same way that entasis was used on ancient Greek and Roman columns. This subtle curvature adds further complication to the task of modelling a bridge!

Finally, to retain the earthworks on each side of the bridge, wing walls were built out from the abutments. They leaned back to counter the thrust of the earth behind, and decreased in size to follow the natural slope of the material. They were capped similarly to the parapet walls, and sometimes ended in a pillar too. They could be straight in plan or curved.

The most straightforward bridge form was the semicircular arch. This type had been in use since Roman times. It was useful where height was not restricted, and has been utilised in viaducts such as the Stour Valley viaduct in Suffolk, but in practice it tended to be chosen for small-span underbridges, such as cattle creeps. The segmental arch was useful for many applications and was particularly suited to multiple-arch viaducts. The semi-elliptical or 'five-centred' arch was ideal for an overbridge giving maximum loading gauge clearance for a minimum of masonry height. It was very popular for use on rural lines such as those in East Anglia.

Rolled Joist Bridges

Perhaps the simplest way of bridging small spans is to lay several beams across to support the deck. This is the function of the rolled joist bridge. The iron, and later steel, was hot-rolled into an 'I' beam, with upper and lower flanges separated by a web. The number varied according to width, the joists being spaced at 2'0" to 2'6" centres, depending on expected loadings. Typically, they were 18" deep. Sometimes the joists were 'pre-stressed'; that is, formed in a low arch, rather than straight.

The gaps between the joists were filled with low arches of brickwork, called 'jack arches', and the decking above was a layer of concrete. Later, from the beginning of the 20th century, concrete played a bigger part in the structure, the brick jack arches making way for precast concrete jack arches, or concrete in iron troughs. Finally the joists themselves were encased in concrete, paving the way for the use of ferro-concrete beams, the favoured method of the present day.

The masonry work in stone or brick associated with arched bridges remained the same for rolled joist bridges. Abutments, parapets, pillars and wing walls still had the same function. Concrete block became increasingly popular, and by the 1910–14 period, it was not unusual to see this type of bridge built entirely of concrete.

Girder Bridges

Beyond a certain span, particularly if there is no height for an arch, the plate girder bridge is the usual solution. The span is carried on two or more beams fabricated from wrought iron or (later) steel. The upper and lower flanges were riveted to the plates forming the web, using right-angle sections, and vertical T stanchions spaced regularly along the span provided stiffening of the web. The flanges were stiffened towards the centre where the bending moment was greatest by progressively adding extra layers of plate. The depth of each girder depended very much on the loading and span, but for spans of 50 to 70 feet typically was in the range 5 to 8 feet. A 25-foot span would only require a depth of around 2 feet.

Spanning between the two main girders were the cross-girders, usually rolled joists. The deck was formed by brick jack arches between the joists, finished off with a layer of concrete. Later, concrete jack arches or iron troughs filled with concrete superseded the brick. Occasionally on underbridges, probably to save dead weight, the decking was omitted, and the rails were carried on 'running timbers' laid directly onto the cross-bearers. Permanent way staff were relegated to using a few planks laid across the beams as a walkway.

The girders were carried on abutments, and where each girder encountered the masonry, a pad of stone or concrete was provided. At each end, pillars of masonry were built just like on a regular bridge, merely to give a visual frame to the public side of the girders.

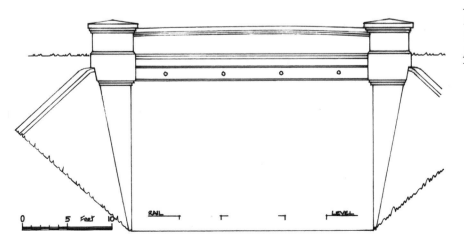

Left: Drawing of a typical rolled iron joist overbridge.

Above: A plate girder bridge over the River Bure, showing the bracing stanchions and thickening of the flanges towards the middle of the span. The span is 50 feet.

Lattice Girder Bridges

Where spans were large, the self-weight of ordinary plate girders would force them to be very deep for their span, making them inefficient and costly, and in these cases lattice girders were used. The members of the girders followed closely the predicted lines of compression and tension and by omitting unnecessary material improved the depth-to-span ratio and produced a beam much lighter than would otherwise be possible. The girders could be arranged as through girders, allowing the trains to run through them, or as under girders, with the trains running over them. Cross bracing was used to knit the two separate beams together to prevent buckling.

There were several different types of lattice girder commonly used. The simplest lattice used a multitude of small-section members arranged in a trellis or 'criss-cross' between an upper and lower flange. The high number of members spread the load and allowed them to be relatively thin. Footbridges on various railways were commonly of this type, but larger viaducts were also constructed, sometimes with latticework piers as well, such as the Great Northern Railway's 1876 Bennerley Viaduct over the Erewash Valley.

The three most common choices for lattice girder bridges were named after their progenitors. Two types of beam were divided up into a number of rectangular sections by vertical stanchions. The Howe truss used struts to brace these sections, the struts acting in compression to carry the loading of the bridge, sloping up from the ends of the girder towards the middle. The Pratt truss used ties acting in tension, the diagonals sloping the opposite way to the Howe truss. Both types often had a crossed pair of diagonals in the centre section. The third type, the Warren truss, rejected the use of vertical ties and retained diagonals only, which can be seen as a series of Ws. The Crumlin Viaduct over Ebbw Vale in Wales had spans of Warren trusses, raised on lattice towers.

Special Bridges

Lattice girder bridges are a relatively small class, but could be incorporated on the average layout. There is an even smaller group of bridges that circumstances have required to be unusual in some way. The most common of these was the swing bridge, which has been included on model railways to good effect, such as 'Sutton Bridge' modelled in 2mm scale, or 'East Lynn' in S Scale. The swinging part is often a lattice girder or other truss type pivoted in the centre on a circular pier, with ordinary girder spans approaching it from each side.

The remaining special types were often very large, and it would be a very special model railway to justify these structures, but they are included for the sake of completeness. The Bowstring or tied-arch girder used an arched top member in compression, supporting the deck below by vertical ties, the deck acting as the tension member to retain the arch in place. The Lenticular arch was a more balanced form of the same phenomenon. Both types of girder are self-contained, exerting no outward thrust on the piers or abutments.

The Forth Bridge is an example of the Cantilever principle, where two girders balance each other on a central support. At the other end of the spectrum, Brunel's timber bridges in Cornwall used a 'fan' of support members springing from tall piers, using the same cantilever principle.

The Box Girder was developed by experimental engineer William Fairbairn, the structural members being arranged into a hollow box cross-section to counter the effects of torsion or twisting under load. They could be used in small sizes under the rails, but the most celebrated applications of the principle were in Stephenson's 'tubular' bridges.

Below: A lattice girder bridge over the River Don on the ex-Great Central Doncaster avoiding line in 1975, with a pair of Class 25s bound for Scunthorpe. The Howe truss bridge beyond is the now-abandoned Hull & Barnsley and GC Joint line, and in the distance are the piers of the A1(M) viaduct. C. P. Boocock, Ian Allan Library

Case Study: Masonry Bridge

For the Brancaster diorama commissioned by Major Henry King, I was engaged to build two bridges and a signalbox, and paint the backscene. The bridge in the centre of the diorama was to be a small masonry occupation bridge. As the layout was to be set on the Great Eastern Railway, I examined several bridges on the local GER line to Cromer and prepared the drawing of a typical segmental arch underbridge seen here. From the drawing, I could sketch a method of construction. The basic carcass of the bridge was to be in 5mm foamboard, with mounting card abutments and intrados. After cutting the materials required, the bridge was assembled, but without the wing walls for the time being.

The exterior walls were clad in Howard Scenic's embossed English bond brick paper. The specially embossed corner strip with queen closers as pressed on one side of each sheet was used at abutment corners, the inevitable join between the two sheets being staggered underneath the arch. A strip corresponding to the rings of the arch was cut away ready to receive the rings. I embossed a sheet of cartridge paper with stretcher bond for the intrados, the ends being folded up over the edge, forming the first ring. The joints naturally had to be snipped here to allow the paper to curve. Three more strips were cut from the Howard Scenic's paper and half-cut at each mortar joint before being glued over the arch to form the other rings. Once the main part of the bridge was finished, the wing walls were added.

The bevel bricks on the string course were made by laying strips of scribed Plastikard over the mounting card former. The bull-nose capping bricks were made by pressing Das clay into a specially made Plastikard mould. The caps to the pillars were all cast in Polyfilla from similar moulds. Each mould was brushed with oil as a releasing agent to allow the cast item to be removed.

Final painting was in acrylic paints. Once dry, a thin mix of light grey matt enamel and white spirit was brushed over, allowed to partially dry, and then the excess removed with a cotton bud, leaving the rest collected in the mortar joints. Using two immiscible forms of paint ensured that one did not dry permanently on the other; a mistake once made, never repeated! Weathering was given by rubbing with black and dark brown pastel crayons, using a finger to smooth it over. This helps the brick colour stand out more from the mortar.

Opposite top:
Finished model of GER underbridge in situ on the diorama. The scenery has not yet been completed. The author painted the backscene as well. L. H. Loveless

Opposite bottom:
Finished model of GER underbridge, showing more of the end pillars. The mileage is painted on the brickwork, a common 19th century practice before cast numberplates became widespread. L. H. Loveless

Below: Drawing of GER segmental underbridge for Major Henry King's diorama.

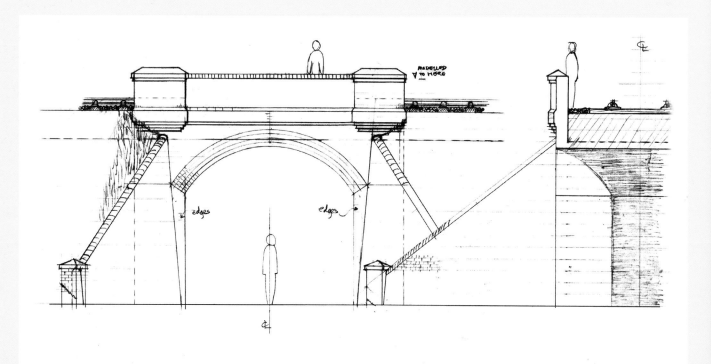

CHAPTER

Passenger Buildings

The main focus for railway modellers, and indeed for us as passengers when considering the railway, is the station. The great difficulty in writing about the British railway station is its variety, as only on relatively few occasions were any two stations identical. It was more common to see perhaps a family resemblance on certain lines, owing to a company style, or the same architect.

One of the problems facing the railway pioneers was that there had never been anything quite like a railway station before. Sometimes a lead was taken from the coaching industry and a room in a nearby house or inn was used to book tickets. On other occasions a more canal-like approach was followed, where the passenger and goods sides of the business shared a warehouse, such as at Liverpool Road in Manchester (1830). The shared approach was very soon perceived as being impractical, and the separation of goods and passengers became the rule.

There was at first no standard model for a passenger station. A terminal station where the station buildings and major circulation area were sited across the end of the tracks, sometimes called a 'head' type, was impressive as a city station, but the buildings could just as easily be at the side on a single platform. This design persisted for smaller-sized termini throughout the railway-building age. Some early practitioners such as Brunel were in favour of the single platform approach even for through stations. A long single platform sited on a loop line catered for Down trains at one end, and Up trains at the other, with a scissors crossing halfway along giving access to the main running lines. With the growth in train services this was found inconvenient, and most stations of this type were rebuilt in the conventional way. The only surviving example still in use today is Cambridge.

Above: The LBSCR rebuilt Bosham (1847) near Chichester in 1902, using the Domestic Revival style. The stretcher bond indicate that much of the building has a cavity wall. J. Scrace, Ian Allan Library

The Standard Station

Once a standard form had been reached, there was quite a rapid evolution, in which the hand of the Board of Trade (later the Ministry of Transport) can be perceived, and a typical form remains in use to this day. On each side of the running lines there obviously had to be a platform. In the first few years, platforms were very low, which suited the rolling stock of the day, but the height was soon increased to the recommended minimum of three feet from the top of the rail. Changes in the brickwork or stonework of platform walls can reveal where a platform has been raised at a later date, and often extended as well, to accommodate longer trains.

On one platform the main offices are located, usually on the side of the line nearest the town or village the station serves. Here would be the ticket office, waiting room, stationmaster's office, and other accommodation for porters, not to mention ladies' and gentlemen's lavatories. Sometimes the stationmaster's house would be part of the building, and according to the period and location of the station, this could be used as an opportunity to make an architectural statement. A number of stations were built on single line, but of course many were on double line, or at passing places, needing a second platform. When this was the case, it became usual to supply a smaller building for passengers there, sometimes little more than an open-fronted shelter, or a standardised shed, particularly if added later. If built in the original design phase of the station, the waiting shelter would usually be in the same style. In larger stations, office accommodation could be included here too.

Below: The Highland Railway also rebuilt many of its stations at the end of the 19th century; Carr Bridge is an example of timber reconstruction. Other rebuilt stations, such as Pitlochry, used stone.
W. A. Sharman,
Ian Allan Library

Above: *Otterington,*
the small North
Eastern Railway
station between
Thirsk and
Northallerton, was
rebuilt in 1933 in
a modern style as
part of the York to
Darlington resignalling.
The Art Deco motif
above the door is
unmistakable. LNER,
Ian Allan Library

An alternative to platforms at the side of the running lines was the island platform, built between the lines. The island platform found particular favour in the latter part of the 19th century. Access to it was often from an overhead station building on a bridge across the site, or from buildings at a lower level with subway access. The Board of Trade urged companies to ensure that movement to and from platforms of all types was made safely with footbridges, but compliance was not universal, and many rural stations had simple boarded foot crossings until recent times. A few still do.

Many of the companies endeavoured to keep their passengers protected to some degree from the elements. At the larger stations and termini this took the form of overall roofs, many of them very elegant constructions of iron and glass. The smaller stations were provided with platform canopies, often quite standardised to a company style, the supporting ironwork exhibiting its initials, or lively designs inspired by nature or heraldry.

At a smaller scale, details are very useful for placing a station in its correct ownership. Most obvious would be the poster and timetable boards, invariably lettered with the owner's title. Platform seats often exhibited company initials in their cast iron supports, or had an identifiable style; the 'rustic' castings of the Midland or the Furness Railways are instantly recognisable. Signage, too, was usually standardised in some way to a company design.

Station Architecture in a Nutshell

What follows is of necessity a highly generalised account of passenger station architecture. There were far too many individual applications of style to say that there was ever a 'typical' station building, but a narrative thread can be dimly perceived. Because of the sheer number of types, photographic examples of some selected stations appear in this chapter and are distributed throughout the book.

As far as architectural style was concerned, until about 1860 there was a willingness to 'pick and mix', but there were four main strands: Tudor, Jacobean, Classical and Italianate, as befitted companies that wanted their buildings to express dignity and reliability. Other more extreme styles such as Gothic and Cottage Orné were present in only a small number of examples.

The Victorian 'Tudor' style often incorporated elements that are more correctly Elizabethan, but it was based on the last medieval style prevalent in this country. It featured low four-centred arches over doorways, steeply pitched roofs, tall decorative chimneys and the distinctive 'dripstone' over mullioned windows. It could be built in brick or stone, but the brick examples invariably had quoins and other detailing in stone.

Jacobean is a term applied to the second English Renaissance style, having elements of the earlier Tudor and Elizabethan periods, but incorporating classical references such as pilasters and round-topped arches, and featuring the ogee-shaped 'Flemish' gable. Roofs were less steep but chimneys were often still tall and decorative. Once again brickwork was usually detailed with stone.

The Classical style is based on Greco-Roman principles of proportion and hierarchy of 'orders', revived in Britain in the 17th century by Inigo Jones using the works of the Italian architect Palladio. At its grandest it involved porticos and pediments, colonnades and pavilions in the approved style, reduced perhaps to Roman arcading and rustication in more modest stations, but being expressed

Below: *The International style of architecture as adapted for Potters Bar station in 1955.* British Railways, Ian Allan Library

more humbly in many stations as a domestic 'Georgian' approach. However, symmetry of composition was important, whatever the scale.

Italianate was inspired by the rustic buildings of the 16th century Italian Renaissance, made popular by the work of Sir Charles Barry. It features low-pitched roofs, often hipped, round-headed windows, and informal asymmetrical façades. A short tower or 'campanile' was often provided on one side. The Italianate style, in one form or another, suited low-cost buildings while retaining some architectural pretensions.

Of all these styles, the only one surviving into the later periods was the Italianate, still being used in the late 19th century. Its longevity produced perhaps the only factor that could be called 'standard' on British railways in the layout of many station buildings. This was the adoption of the pavilion-style plan, in which a larger block was paired with a similar block, sometimes the same size but often smaller, the two separated by a low range of offices between.

As well as the survival of the Italianate, the 1860s saw the emergence of more standardised company architecture. This was not necessarily universally applied to all of a particular company's lines, there frequently being new designs for each line built, but obvious similarities did appear, such as the use of company-specific bargeboards or platform canopies. The London & North Western, for example, designed a distinctive standard timber station, erected from pre-assembled components. Generally, the approach was simplified, with less reference to historical details and plainer styling. Perhaps the most consistent standardisation of station architecture could be seen on the Great Central Railway's London Extension of 1899.

In parallel with the company designs and Italianate style, the 1860s to the 1880s saw a vogue in the use of 'French Renaissance' for large stations and their hotels, giving them a resemblance to a French château. A symmetrical plan having highly decorated elevations was topped with straight-sided or bulbous mansard roofs, often with cast iron cresting. A clock and a porte-cochère were usually present too.

From the late 1880s until about 1910 the fashion among many of Britain's railways was for the Domestic Revival. This had its roots in English vernacular architecture and featured half-timbered gables, tiled roofs and large chimneys. Windows often had upper panes divided into smaller squares or rectangles. Larger stations in the first two decades of the 20th century rejected this domestic scale for opulent Edwardian Baroque, with highly decorated stonework or flamboyant terracotta.

The years after the First World War were those of the Grouping, where most of the dozens of individual companies were absorbed into four grouped companies. For new construction in this period a sort of corporate neo-Georgian was universal, the Great Western favouring a Portland stone ashlar cladding. The first hints of modernism appeared in 1929, championed by the Underground system in London. The Art Deco styling, vertical glazing and clean, geometric shapes combined into what has become dubbed the 'Odeon' style after the contemporary cinemas of that name.

After the devastation of World War 2, a period of rebuilding in strictly utilitarian fashion gave way to the adoption of the International style of modern architecture in the more optimistic 1950s, with some very successful examples. In the 1960s the style degenerated with the emergence of a corporate British Rail approach of system cladding under heavy slab-like roofs. There are too many examples to mention, but surely the word 'Euston' conjures up the unhappy state of railway architecture in the 60s. However, it must be said that the design of the new BR emblem or logo I consider to be a triumph, and is still recognisable today, but the simultaneous adoption of the lower-case Helvetica typeface for station names was (in my view) a dismal failure.

After the retrenchment and pessimism of the 1970s, the 80s and 90s saw the emergence of a post-modern style of British railway architecture, using dark red-brown brick and low-pitched machine-made slate roofs with large overhangs. However, over the past three or four decades, the onus seems to have been more on demolition, and replacement by buildings that are little more than bus-shelters. This means that the fabric of our railway architectural heritage has been immeasurably weakened. Fortunately, many stations are now Listed Grade II status, and some of them Grade I, which arguably gives them a less uncertain future.

Case Study: Cromer Beach Station

For the Cromer Project, a 7mm reconstruction of Cromer Beach station in 1912 by my friend Lawrie Loveless, I was commissioned to build a windmill, the goods shed, the water tower, the loco shed and the station building. Of these, by far the largest was the station building. As usual, the starting point was a good set of drawings. Fortunately, the M&GN Circle has a great many drawings, including the original ones done by William Marriott himself, plus of course the station itself is only just down the road from where I live.

From a combination of these drawings, a number of photographs of the station through the years, and site visits, a completely new set of drawings was prepared in 7mm scale. On a tangent, this initial stage also prompted me to research enamel advertising signs, as I had a list of the signs present but few details, and the signs would be an important factor in the historical accuracy of the period depicted. My results were later published in *British Railway Modelling*.

The first step would be the marking out and cutting of the mounting board carcass. I decided against using foamcore board, as the window and door reveals were small and trying to fit windows at the correct depth would have added an unnecessary complication. I also decided against adding prototypical thickness to the walls. To save time, I painted internal finishes and doors directly to the rear of the structural members. Fortunately, the Howard Scenic's embossed English bond brick card (thicker than the paper) did not cause the walls to warp when it was glued on the carcass.

The building is in the Domestic Revival style popular in the late 19th century (Cromer Beach was opened in 1887). It is long, but actually quite narrow, so the floor area is not great. At the western end of the main building is the stationmaster's house, with ancillary buildings beyond. At the eastern end is the refreshment room with the restaurant above. The upper floors at both ends jetty out slightly, so these were made as separate boxes. Once the carcass was cut out, floors were

Below: *Cromer Beach station photographed in 1914.* L&GRP, author's collection

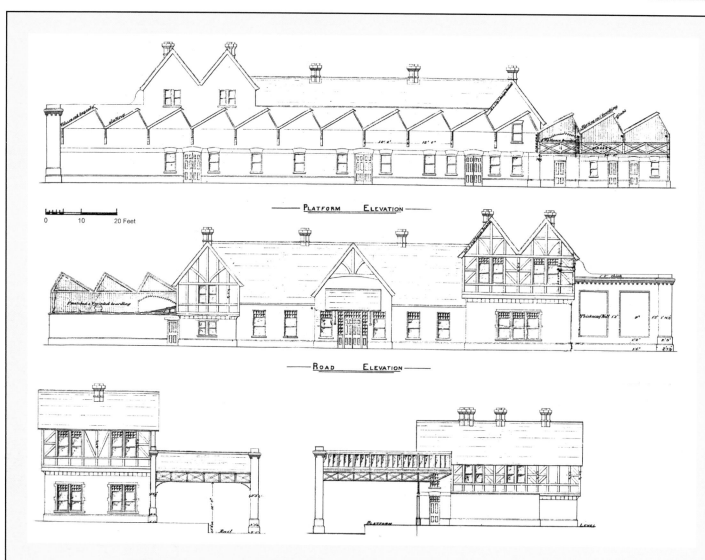

PLATFORM ELEVATION

0   10   20 Feet

ROAD ELEVATION

Above: Drawing of Cromer Beach, compiled from the original 1886 contract drawings.

painted to represent wood, walls were painted cream, with brown up to dado level. Internal doors and ticket windows were painted on, too. The various parts were assembled, leaving the upper floors separate and the roofs unfixed.

Then came the task of cutting and fitting the embossed brick card, making sure all corners were correct. The eastern end featured a thick blank wall supporting the end of the train shed, having many details such as a dentil course and a capping of very large special blue bricks arranged in a 'Dutch' curve up to the roof of the restaurant.

The upper floors are 'half-timbered' so each timber frame member was fabricated from Plastikard and mounted onto the card carcass. The gaps between were infilled with Polyfilla to represent the stucco, except the lowest parts, which were filled with diagonal brick courses. Painting followed, mostly local red brick, but yellow brick featured on the wall facing the train shed, and blue bevel bricks throughout. The mortar was represented by my usual method of diluted light grey Humbrol being washed on, allowed to partially dry, and the excess removed with cotton buds. The timber frames were painted the standard M&GN tan colour.

The next process was to make the doors and windows. The doors were simple enough, but the dozens of windows were all sash, and some had coloured glass upper panes. I made each window as a unit mounted in its frame, with upper and lower sashes properly separate. Here I made a decision which I now regret; I used clear Plastikard as the glazing material. I should have used polycarbonate, as although it is thick, it at least has the saving grace of being rigid. After 10 years, most of the Plastikard windows have bowed slightly, not disastrously, but still annoying to me, the builder. The colours for the upper lights on many of the public

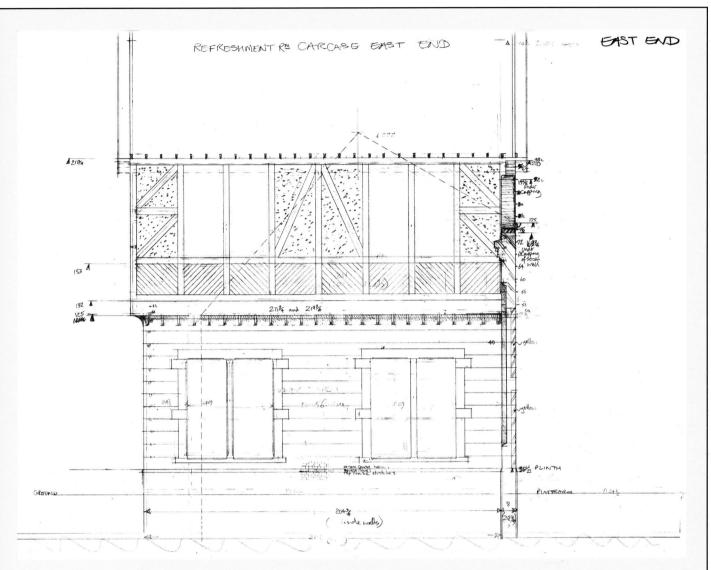

Above: One of the working drawings in 7mm scale prepared for the model.

windows were surmised from similar windows on a surviving platform waiting shelter at Raynham Park station, where three colours are used: amber, lilac and green. Squares of the right size were cut out from stage lighting gels before being glued in place. All the window sashes and frames were painted light grey rather than white, which is too bright at this scale. Doors were painted the usual M&GN two-tone tan and buff.

After the windows and doors were fitted, final assembly could take place. All interior details were completed first, including two staircases, bar area, restaurant tables, lavatory cubicles, ticket office and waiting room. Notices and pictures were added where appropriate, and a table with a potted plant were provided in the ladies' waiting room. Some period figures were set in place, and a few discreet bulbs for lighting. Open window sashes, curtains (tissue paper) and calico window blinds (brown paper), some drawn down against the glare of the summer sun, were fitted in accordance with photographs taken in 1914. The various parts were glued together, leaving only the roof unfixed.

The roof was marked out to give the positioning of the tile courses, before being glued to the main building. The bargeboards, fascia boards and gutters were then fixed and painted M&GN tan, with dark grey inside the gutters. The chimneys were based on card boxes, finished with brick card and extra layers to give the corbelling of the brick courses, before being painted, mortared and weathered and fixed in place. All was now ready for the repetitive business of adding strip after strip of half-cut card to represent the roof tiles. Ridge tiles were bent up from card and their cockscombs were cut from Plastikard, which I hoped

Right: *The first stage of building Cromer Beach, the carcass.*

would give them strength. Painting and weathering followed. Lead flashing was added using aluminium foil.

My attention could now turn to the screen wall and train shed. I had already made the carcass of the screen wall, using foamcore board. Fortunately, I did not have to worry about making the windows for this part, 14 in total, as I had prepared drawings of them, plus all the spandrels and lattice girders inside the train shed, and Lawrie had them all etched. Each window frame was in two parts, inner and outer, which I painted tan and then mounted clear Plastikard between them. The brick card was mounted on the outside of the screen wall first to give the correct reveal, and then the windows were fixed against this from the inside. The inner brick card was added last. The pads supporting the ends of the train shed girders were then attached at the correct height. Painting followed in the usual way.

Before proceeding further, the whole station was mounted onto a chipboard baseboard, and the platform attached and surfaced with card cut to represent York stone. Details such as platform seats, poster boards and enamel signs were fitted now, before the train shed would be nearly inaccessible under its roof. The screen wall was fixed in place, allowing the pre-painted girders and E&MR spandrels to be dropped into position. Once the metalwork was fixed, I could then build up the 'northlight' roof with card and Plastikard glazing. The plain side of each roof was slate, except the last one which, being visible to the public, was tiled to match the rest of the station. Once again I added the cockscomb ridges with cut Plastikard. Lead flashing in aluminium foil finished off each side of the roof.

The glazed canopy to the front doors was made very much by copying the construction of the original; I could see no other way to do it. Therefore a card frame was made just like the timber one. Glazing was cut and glued to it in two sheets, an upper and a lower. Glazing bars were added from Plastikard microstrip before the flashing along the hips. The M&GN spandrels were once again etched and soldered by Lawrie, leaving me to fabricate some columns from brass tube with added details, such as an octagonal lower portion. Once painted, married up with the canopy and glued in place, the flashing to the wall could be added in the usual way.

The final fitting was to attach all the rainwater downpipes on the station, and there were a lot of them! The 13 on the outside of the train shed have rainwater hoppers, and Lawrie helped here again by having them cast in white metal to a pattern I made. After the addition of a poster board, a sign advertising the refreshment room in Art Nouveau lettering, and adding a roadway, some cellar doors by the refreshment rooms and more York stone paving, the station was finished.

Above: *The model from the stationmaster's house, looking towards the restaurant.*

Left: *The front entrance and canopy. Note the M&GN initials in the spandrels.*

Above: The model from a similar viewpoint as the 1914 photograph.

Right: The interior of the train shed, with all the enamel signs, poster boards and seats. Enamel signs are a vital component of the railway scene before the 1930s, when paper adverts replaced most of them.

Right: *The exterior of the train shed, showing the northlight roof and decorative screen wall.*

Left: *The Third Class Ladies' Waiting Room, an addition to the original construction.*

Goods Buildings

Goods facilities could vary considerably, from a single siding alongside a passenger platform, to vast warehouses on several floors served by many tracks all interconnected with wagon turntables. Wagon turntables were used extensively in these urban situations and the later large bogie wagons were always given free-rotating bogies so that they could still be shunted in this way.

In the large conurbations, goods stations tended to be separate from passenger areas, and also had their functions separated, particularly in London. Cattle would be dealt with at the great Metropolitan Cattle Market at Caledonian Road; coal would be delivered to dedicated coal depots, leaving the general merchandise to be handled in closed warehouses. This could also be true at provincial cities, for example Norwich. The GER and later the LNER were fortunate to have, through an accident of history, two termini at Norwich. Thorpe (in the east) was the station that handled passenger traffic and merchandise. The smaller Victoria (to the south) was the main coal depot, and Trowse, the first station out of Thorpe on the London line, was the livestock depot. As a contrast, the M&GN's City station, although the largest in area on the joint line, had all the goods business concentrated at the same site.

Below: A typical city goods warehouse, seen here at Heaton Norris depot (ex-LNWR) in Stockport. The wagon turntables are visible, and one of the powered capstans used for shunting wagons by rope. T. Lewis, Ian Allan Library

The Goods Yard

Out in the suburban areas and generally throughout the country, the open siding was the rule. The amount of siding space and other facilities depended on the thinking of the railway company. Some stations were made in a smaller size to meet a modest expectation of traffic – after all, enlargement could come in time – but others were deliberately made with generous provision in order to encourage traffic and even to expand the community. This did indeed often happen.

In these open yards, sidings were usually paired, meaning that two lines of wagons could be attended to in an economical width. The goods yard would be approached through a set of gates, beside which were often the weigh office and weighbridge. Where the goods office was not part of the goods shed, this was usually nearby. The yard was divided into nominal areas where various functions occurred.

The most important siding area in rural stations up and down the country would be for coal traffic. One or more sidings would be allocated to the private coal depots of traders, for which they would pay siding rent. There were thousands of traders on the railway system, and their wagons can be found in various publications (see Bibliography). Coal was deposited in heaps on the traders' coal grounds; the serried ranks of 'coal staithes' are largely a myth perpetrated by modellers, although they were more common in the postwar period. Coal stacking, the art of building walls of coal to contain the heap, was the preferred method of long-term storage. All that the trader would have was a small office and perhaps some low timber walls to delineate his boundary. The NER was the only railway to consistently supply coal drops at its rural stations.

Above: The Great Western Railway goods shed at Taplow. The GWR was fond of timber goods sheds. The loading gauge has been incorporated into the shed structure.
K. Williams,
Ian Allan Library

Cattle were another important rural traffic. The amount of cattle handled at any station depended very much on local conditions, but most stations would have had one or two pens, and some considerably more, particularly if there were a weekly cattle market at that place. Their position in the goods yard was not standardised, but they were almost invariably provided with their own entrance and cattle drove. Beside the pens would be a hut containing sawdust and lime. The lime would be slaked with water and used to wash down the whole area to prevent the spread of disease. The sawdust was put in the wagons to absorb droppings. The cattle area would stand out a stark white against the drab areas of the rest of the yard, until the 1930s, when lime was replaced by disinfectants, which were colourless.

Merchandise that could make up a full wagonload was loaded or unloaded directly at the rail side. This included many of the products of agriculture such as potatoes, sacks of grain, fruit and hay, or products of local industry such as fish, manufactured items and kegs of beer. Large items such as timber or metal castings were also handled here. A crane would be required for this, but many stations did not have one, or had one of insufficient bearing capacity, so one of the company's travelling cranes would be sent to deal with the item. Any goods loaded in the yard would have to pass beneath the loading gauge, which could be set for various heights to ensure that the loaded wagons could safely traverse the lines for which they were bound.

Wheeled loads, such as private carriages, motorcars, or traction engines were loaded onto carriage trucks or machine trucks and shunted to the end-loading dock, which many stations possessed. This was often a fenced-off part of the main platform, and was provided with hinged metal plates, which could bridge the gap between dock and wagon to enable the vehicle to be unloaded.

The Goods Shed

The merchandise that was not in full wagon loads was dealt with in the goods shed. This traffic would later be called 'sundries'. A great deal of the non-mineral goods traffic on any railway was of this nature, where many different packages or crates from different consignors were loaded into 'road vans' for one destination. These were not special vehicles, but ordinary vans or sheeted open wagons. The merchandise would be unloaded and wait to be delivered by the railway, or collected by the consignee, depending on the rate paid. Similarly, the shed would be used to store items before they could be loaded into road vans for other destinations. Sometimes, where the traffic justified it, a special goods shed for grain only was provided. One or more grain merchants would hire the floor space and conduct their business from there. In fact several coal merchants were grain merchants as well.

The working area inside a goods shed would be divided up into sectors allocated to various destinations, both on the railway system and for delivery to the community at large, where the packages would be piled. To assist movement of heavier items, internal cranes were often a feature, usually a simple hand crane able to lift one ton.

Where a full wagon could not be achieved for one destination, and there was no road van available, several destinations would be combined in one wagon, and marked 'tranships'. The wagon would be sent to the nearest tranship shed, where packages for one destination would be combined with others sent from similar stations, to make up a full load. These tranship sheds were little different from a goods shed, except that road access was not required, and at least two lines of rails were usually provided to make wagon-to-wagon transfer easier.

Goods sheds were naturally built in many styles, using brick, stone or timber, but most of them shared the feature of a covered area or a through siding to allow protection from the weather. The sizes varied according to local expectations; some were barely larger than a modern garden shed, others were huge, sometimes dwarfing the modest passenger facilities. After the initial pioneering phase of

railway building, goods sheds were usually built to standardised drawings issued from the company's architect's office and can often be used in photographs to identify a company, or at least a likely location.

Tariff Sheds

A type of small goods shed not often modelled is the tariff shed. These were essentially small 'lock-ups', usually positioned at the rear of the main platform of a station with no other goods shed. They would store smaller single items presented to the railway for transit, similar to parcels, but at the lower goods rates. These would be put into the brake van, a wagon on the goods train specified for 'tariffs', or even a special tariff wagon or tariff brake van. The tariffs would be grouped together into road vans at the local tranship sheds. Those items for wayside stations would be separated again at a tranship shed near their destination, and put off as tariffs from the goods trains when they called there.

Just as for the main buildings, the materials for construction could vary, from timber, to brick or concrete block. On the M&GN, the original contractor built a species of tariff shed from timber with a monopitch roof.

Above: The interior of Wellingborough goods shed (MR) in 1979, showing the hand crane and the timber bracing above. The door to the goods office is beyond. R. Payne, Ian Allan Library

Above: The tariff shed at Honing (M&GN) in 1902. Note the padlock. Briston Archive Trust, courtesy Ray Meek

The Goods Office

A railway generated mountains of paperwork for the goods staff, with all of its invoices, delivery notes, demurrage registers and the like. Nothing was ever knowingly destroyed; foreign wagon labels had to be kept for a year before being sent to storage. To accommodate all this activity, a goods office was essential. In many cases it was attached to the goods shed, but not invariably. In it, the clerks would receive the wagon labels and the invoices behind them from the yard staff, and then make out delivery notes for the road drivers, or postcards to be sent to the consignee to tell them their goods were ready for pickup. Copies of everything were kept using the wet press method. A fireplace would be needed, as a goods yard can be a cold place during the winter.

Weighbridges

Many stations had a weighbridge, on which drays and later lorries could stand. By subtracting the tare weight of the vehicle from the gross weight, the load could be calculated, and the amount put in each wagon known. The location for the weighbridge and its associated office was usually by the yard gates. Standardised drawings were issued for these buildings, and it is easy to identify a Midland example, for instance.

Above: The goods office at Cromer Beach in 1902, before a weighbridge was installed. In the background is the goods shed and crane. Briston Archive Trust, courtesy Ray Meek

Left: The weighbridge hut at Hawes (Midland and North Eastern Joint) is typical of the breed, although the usual choice of material was brick. D. Pennington, Ian Allan Library

Above:

A replacement for the horse, the Scammell 'mechanical horse', pauses with its trailer for weighing at the Falkner Street entrance of Crown Street goods depot, Liverpool, in the 1950s.
British Railways, Ian Allan Library

Smaller country stations often had to do without a weighbridge and in these cases, merchandise was weighed on smaller scales, or a wagon would be loaded and sent with a 'TO WEIGH' label to the nearest station with a rail weighbridge so that its weight could be known, and any excess load transferred to another wagon.

Collection and Delivery

For payment of a higher rate, the railway company would collect and/or deliver your items for you. A large collection of drays, vans and other road vehicles was required for this work, originally all horse-drawn. To accommodate the horses, most stations where collection and delivery was advertised had stables. The large stable block at Norwich City goods station was typical of the type, accommodation for 24 horses being arranged around a yard with plenty of roof ventilation. Here, the vehicles not in use were parked along the wall, but in large conurbations a dedicated depot for road vehicles was common.

There were early attempts to supplement or replace horses with steam, electric and petrol road vehicles, but it was not until the 1920s that motor vehicles began

to make a serious contribution. By the late 1930s and the introduction of many different types of motor lorry including the iconic Scammell 'mechanical horse', the number of railway horses had dropped significantly. Even so, they were still present in the 1950s.

In rural districts, the railway companies usually subcontracted a local carrier to conduct the collection and delivery work for them, rather than have the expense of housing a horse and dray at each station. Most traffic other than sundries in these areas would be agricultural anyway, and brought in to the station on the farmer's own transport.

Above: Modern container goods handling. This is Follingsby Freightliner terminal, near Washington, Tyne & Wear. I. S. Carr, Ian Allan Library

Case Study: Cromer Goods Shed

The goods shed at Cromer Beach was a complete contrast to the station. Where the latter was full of internal walls, lending stability to the whole building, the goods shed was simply one open space, with no bracing other than the floor and the roof. Fortunately the dimensions were relatively small, 52'6" × 23'6" scaling to 367.5mm × 164.5mm overall, but large door openings would weaken the structure. Because of this, and also because of the wall thickness (14" with panels of 9" brickwork internally), I used foamcore board as the main carcass.

Cutting and assembling the main walls was simple enough, with layers of mounting board to increase the thickness where required. I assembled the whole building on a baseboard of 1/8in obechi. The internal floor was raised on a platform of card, and because it was laid in blue brick paviors, I had to scribe it with stretcher bond myself. The Howard Scenic's embossed brick paper was added next, taking particular care around the door openings, as I wanted the doors to be fully functional and the brickwork could potentially be seen all round. It was a new experience for me applying brick paper *inside* a building. At this stage, the walls were painted, mortared and weathered. External brick was the local red variety, with some blue brick edges and plinth brick, and blue brick flooring. Internally I painted the walls light grey, to represent whitewash.

The roof was cut from mounting board, but as the interior would be visible to the roof, I cut out and mounted nine simple representations of the roof trusses, five of which extended beyond the walls to support a canopy on the roadside elevation. Bargeboards and fascias were added, but the roof was left as a separate module for the time being.

Returning to the building, a timber loading platform built from card and small section pine was added along the railside elevation, and a blue brick pad with a timber extension to take a 1 ton hand crane. The crane has yet to be researched and built. The large end window was put in at this stage, made from a double skin of Plastikard pre-painted tan on the outside and light grey on the inside, holding the glazing between. The three sliding doors were also embossed, cut out from mounting board, painted and made to slide with Plastikard brackets along small channel section Plastruct. Once all the access to the interior was complete, I permanently attached the roof.

To complete the roof section, I constructed the screen wall which protected the railside elevation from the weather. I drew the framework out and assembled the

Right: Model of Cromer Beach goods shed in 7mm scale, showing the roadside elevation and the base for the crane. The sliding doors are fully functional.
L. H. Loveless

Right: Drawing of Cromer Beach goods shed.

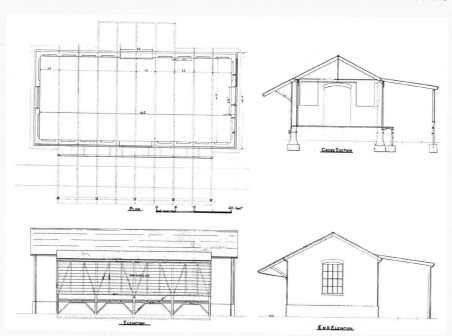

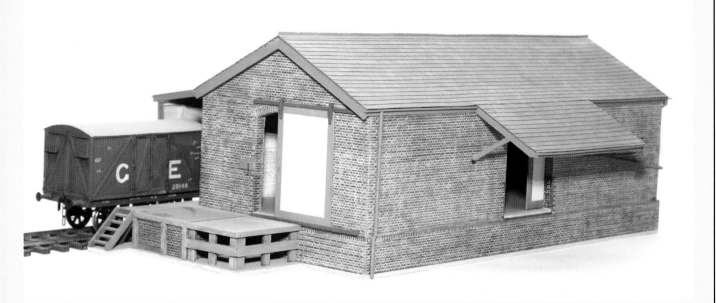

strips of pine section actually on the drawing. The external weatherboard cladding I added from strips of Plastikard. The roof was an unknown quantity, but I assumed it was clad in zinc or lead sheeting battened together and treated it accordingly. To make it more simple to mount the goods shed on the layout, I kept the screen as a separate entity, the join with the main roof covered by a flashing. To make the vulnerable joint more sturdy, I used paper for the flashing instead of my usual aluminium foil. Once the flashing was in place, I could finish off the roof with slating cut in strips from thin card, topped with ridge tiles which I folded up from the same card.

Final fittings were the fire buckets and warning sign, the gutters and downpipes, and the simple door latches.

Above: Cromer Beach goods shed in 7mm scale from the railside, showing the canopy protecting the loading doors and the fire buckets. L. H. Loveless

Buildings for Signalling and Permanent Way

5

The Signalbox

The buildings that can be classed as signalboxes first started appearing in the 1850s and a decade later had reached a form recognisable as such today. The original boxes were designed by the signal manufacturing companies, but railway companies themselves introduced their own designs during the 1870s and 80s, many of them very distinctive and an indicator of the owning company, which is a good way to set the scene on a model railway. Signalboxes were positioned at the ends of block sections, guarding the entrance to the next section, and wherever else signals were needed. Therefore, almost every station, junction, goods siding or other location where the main running lines were joined by other lines had a signal box, which makes them vital to the built environment of your railway. Although there were differences between signal boxes in both size and design, these were only of a superficial nature, and the actual basic form of a typical box remained the same across the British Isles and indeed worldwide. For a more detailed analysis of the signalbox and its function, the reader should consult the companion volume in this series: *Aspects of Modelling: Railway Signalling.*

Below: A timber signalbox. The standard Midland Railway Type 2b box at Attenborough (shortened to Attenboro' on the nameboard) near Nottingham. Note the details of the level crossing gates, the lamps and the signs.
Ian Allan Library

The position of a signalbox depended very much on the location and the date of its construction. In the early days of signalling, only 150 yards was allowed by the Board of Trade for control rods, so many boxes were central between two loop points or crossovers. This often resulted in a signalbox being built on the platform. The alternative was to build two signalboxes, one at each end of the location. Relaxation of the rules in 1892 and 1925 allowed many of these second boxes to be removed, or central ones to be abolished. The archetypal position for a box thereafter was at the end of a platform, and where there was a level crossing at the station, the box would usually be adjacent to that. Where this was not possible, a small gate cabin would be provided, locked from the box.

The length of a signalbox mostly depended on the number of levers in the frame, plus space on either side for access to the windows and for other equipment. The normal length of box in a location not requiring special treatment would have been between 15 and 25 feet. Widths did not vary much from between 10 and 13 feet. Height was a more variable commodity. One of the most fundamental requirements, particularly in the early days before electrical repeaters, was the ability of the signalman to see his signals. For this reason the operating floor of the signalbox was usually elevated to give the signalman a good view. Eight feet from ground to floor was a normal figure, but the conditions at a particular location sometimes resulted in a very tall building or, conversely, a very short one. Staircases allowed access to the operating floor, usually being wooden ones on the outside, but sometimes they were provided internally. Below the operating

Above: An example of 'brick-to-floor' construction on the London & North Western Railway at Eastwood's Sidings. This box is of the LNWR Type 5, a design used from 1904 to the Grouping. V. R. Anderson, Ian Allan Library

Above: *The Great Western Type 7a signalbox at Midgham illustrates the 'brick' construction. This design of box was in use on the GWR from 1896 to 1925, but this particular subgroup dates from the first four or five years.* D. E. Canning, Ian Allan Library

floor was a room almost invariably termed the 'locking room'. This often did contain the locking frame associated with the lever frame, but some designs of frame had the locking at operating floor level. The room contained the batteries that powered the electrical equipment, the lever 'tails' and the rods, chains and cranks from them to the outside world.

The material used to build the signalbox varied considerably. Nearly half of all signalboxes were built in timber. This could be because the signalling department had designed a standard box which could be erected anywhere, or it was considered to be a cheaper alternative to brick. Site considerations played a part too. On embankments or areas with unstable ground, the lighter timber construction was the natural choice.

The main alternative to timber was brick. Very little signalbox construction used local stone, and this was mostly confined to the West and the North of Britain. Concrete or concrete block was represented by very few examples. Brick was used in a number of ways, identified by the Signalling Study Group: 'brick to floor' (brick to operating floor level, timber above, occasionally brick rear wall); 'brick' (brick up to window cills, and rear wall, but timber around and above windows); and 'brick to roof' (only the window frames are timber). The most common, with about a third of all examples, was the 'brick' type.

To aid visibility, a signalbox would usually have large windows at the front and sides. These were of varying sizes and styles, depending on the company. Apart from the North British and the South Eastern Railways, which preferred standard vertical sash windows, the usual arrangement was for signalboxes to have sliding horizontal sash windows. These allowed a flow of air, very important in summer when the glass had a greenhouse effect, and permitted the signalman to speak to train crews or to give hand signals. They also allowed access to the fixed lights for cleaning, and often gave a route onto a walkway arranged at cill level around the glazed portions of the building for the same function. Many companies just provided a grabrail for the signalman to hold on to, but others provided safety railings.

The interior of a signalbox is an important aspect of the modelled building, being seen through the large windows. The lever frame would typically be at the front, with a block shelf above it carrying the block instruments, repeaters and bells required. Over the block shelf was the framed signalling diagram for the location. At the side of the lever frame and standing on the floor would be the single line instruments if required, and a gatewheel if the signalbox controlled a level crossing. At the rear would be the lockers for storage, the train register desk and the stove or fireplace. On the wall would be a noticeboard for the weekly notices and other operating changes received from the Traffic Manager's Office, and a framed print of the gradient diagram for the line. Overlooking the scene was the clock.

Roofs were usually gabled, although some railways and manufacturers preferred hipped roofs. The roofs were almost invariably slated. Tile was not favoured until after the Grouping. The Highland Railway used corrugated iron as standard. Bargeboards on gabled roofs were often decorated, and these designs

Below: The 'brick-to-roof' style as shown by the Southern Railway's modern style at Bognor Regis. The roof and lintels for the doors and windows are reinforced concrete. J. Scrace, Ian Allan Library

could be an indicator of ownership or manufacturer. Wooden spike finials were very popular.

Where stoves were provided for heating, the stovepipe would penetrate the roof with lead flashing to prevent water leakage. Older boxes, particularly brick ones, often had fireplaces rather than stoves, with proper chimneys. Near the box would be ancillary features such as coal and ash bins, and the oil and lamp hut. If not at a station, an earth closet for the signalman would be a necessity. Very few box types incorporated a room for the closet, and it was usual for it to be in a small hut near the foot of the steps. A water butt collected rainwater where there was no piped water available.

With the move from mechanical signalling to the route-setting panel, signalboxes deviated from the traditional form and joined the mainstream of corporate railway architecture. Flat roofs became the norm, and as panel boxes controlled larger and larger districts, windows from which to see trains and signals became redundant. The modern Integrated Electronic Control Centre (IECC) has no need of them and resembles a windowless office building more than a signalbox.

Associated with the signalboxes were fog huts. These simple timber structures resembled a sentry box, and when not in use were laid on the ground, front down. Men were stationed by the distant signals in fog or falling snow to place detonators on the rail when the signals were at 'caution', and these huts were supplied to give the men some degree of shelter. Advances in 20th century signalling gradually removed the need for them.

Gatehouses and Level Crossings

Public road crossings were of course a necessary evil. To reduce road crossings to a minimum, engineers aimed their line for crossroads or other junctions, a simple road deviation reducing several possible road crossings to one. The Parliamentary plans had to detail these road deviations and also how much the public road needed to be raised or lowered. In urban areas it was not as easy to divert or stop up roads, and so crossings tended to be more numerous. Housing and roads built after the railway tended to be dead-ends or cul-de-sacs.

Not all crossings were for public use. Occupation crossings were negotiated with the landowners whose land the line passed through, to allow private roads to cross the line, or for them to be able to reach parts of their property isolated by the passage of the railway. Footpaths may also have had rights of way across the route. If the crossing was a bridge, then this is dealt with in Chapter Three. However, bridges contributed heavily to the construction costs and away from main lines, railways tended to go for the cheapest option – a level crossing.

Level crossings were a mixed blessing. On one hand, the company was saved the cost of a bridge, but on the other there was need for constant vigilance and staffing. Some level crossings were controlled from adjacent signalboxes, being opened by mechanical means, but many on rural lines were opened by hand. The Board of Trade urged railway companies to protect all such crossings with distant signals, operated from a ground frame near the gates and interlocked with them. Despite this, many remained unprotected, and there were inevitably cases of gates being run through. The engineering department kept a store of gates ready for rapid replacement in case of accident, but there was no guarantee that a matching gate could be found, so mismatches were not uncommon.

The gates themselves were relatively standard in form. The timber outer frame was divided into rectangles by vertical members, which were then cross-braced. The timber was always dressed off nicely at the edges with chamfers, and invariably painted white. The differences were in the detail, some companies preferring a round red-painted warning 'target', others a diamond shape, some preferring horizontal safety bars across the open spaces, others vertical. Mounted on the top of the gates were lamps presenting a red warning light when across both road and railway. Beside the gates, if a ground frame was employed to

operate distant signals and unlock the gates, a small crossing cabin would often be found.

Length of gate varied according to the crossing. A square crossing, with the road and double line of railway at right angles would require two gates per side of 14 feet, or one of 28 feet. It was more usual for gates operated from a signalbox to be the paired variety. The long gates would be kept horizontal by a tie rod from a tall hanging post. Minor roads over one line of railway would require only one gate per side. If the roadway were at an angle to the railway, then the extra length would require longer or paired gates. There were often small wicket gates at one side of the main gates for pedestrians to use, these remaining open after the main gates had been shut, until the train was nearer and the signalman would lock them.

The material forming the surface of the crossing varied. A popular choice was to use redundant sleepers. Metal plates could also be employed. Occasionally in more recent times, the tar-and-chippings metalling of the road surface was simply carried over the crossing. Concrete precast sections are now almost universal.

The crossing keeper was often the wife of a permanent way man, whose family lived in the gatehouse. Gatehouses were provided at crossings not operated by signalboxes in accordance with Acts of Parliament of 1839 and 1845, which required supervision of all public crossings. It is important to remember that, unless otherwise ordered by the Board of Trade (and later the Ministry of

Above: *A lonely gatehouse at Bramfield near Halesworth on the East Suffolk line. Hundreds of public roads were protected by simple arrangements such as this.*
Ian Allan Library

Transport), level crossing gates were normally closed across the roadway until needed to open to allow vehicles to pass. In practice, if a train was not due for some time, crossing keepers would probably leave the gates open once having been asked to open them, but legally they were not obliged to do so. Bells and repeaters of the instruments from the signal boxes on either side warned them of any track occupancy.

Gatehouses were not of a universal type, but they were usually small. Some railway companies, or the contractors that built them, preferred two-storey dwellings, others a single-storey 'bungalow'. Their repetition along a particular line was guaranteed, and can set the scene for a chosen location very well. As an example, on the M&GN there were three main types. The earliest were the simple narrow two-storey dwellings with gabled roofs and a canopy over the door, used on the Spalding line. A second type, a single-storey cottage with a hipped roof and a porch, was used on the Peterborough to Sutton Bridge line. On the Eastern Section from King's Lynn to Yarmouth and Norwich, a very simple bungalow with two rooms under a pitched slate roof was used, with distinctive curved bargeboards and a rear kitchen. Use of one of these three types immediately places the model in the appropriate section of the M&GN, and a similar mechanism would be in operation on the lines of other railways.

Above: Billingham signalbox and level crossing on the OO gauge layout of the Middlesbrough Model Railway Club. Tony Wright, courtesy British Railway Modelling

In 1954, British Railways was allowed to begin installing lifting barriers as a substitution for the traditional gates. Three years later, an Act of Parliament removed the need for gatekeepers at every crossing by authorising the use of automatic activation, or activation by remote control from a distant signalbox. Full-width barriers with safety skirts were the first design applied, but from 1961 the automatic half-barrier was introduced. All through the 1960s, 70s and 80s, the traditional gated crossing was replaced by the new designs, so that few now remain.

Occupation crossings were usually provided with a surface boarded using redundant sleepers. Gates of the traditional 12-foot-long 'field gate' type were provided, hinged to open away from the railway and adorned with cast iron notices reminding the person crossing to 'SHUT THIS GATE' or similar warnings. The gates and gateposts were invariably painted white. Signs nearby warned the user to beware of trains and not to trespass on the railway.

Lineside Huts

Every railway line was divided into permanent way lengths, each maintained by a p/w gang. Each gang of four or five men would have about 3 or 4 miles of line to look after, a material stacking area, and at least one hut on their length. The stacking area, usually in an obscure corner of a station yard, would be kept very clean and tidy, as was the entire length. Huts were similar over most of the railway system, usually being laid out parallel with the track, with a door at one end, a chimney at the other and a window to one side. Bench seats were provided along each wall. Materials used were timber, brick and (later) concrete block. Timber huts tended to be sleepers butted together, their joints covered by small square section battens, and often had monopitch roofs, sloping to the rear, and fireplaces and chimneys built of brick. Brick examples usually had gabled roofs, again with a chimney. Occasionally, withdrawn rolling stock was pressed into service.

Concrete block huts were introduced during the second decade of the 20th century, and at first merely copied the standard brick format, until a precast concrete sectional building system was evolved by the LNER in the 1930s. The Southern also had a concrete sectional standard hut. BR continued the use of the concrete sectional system until recent years, but now the ubiquitous 'portakabin' and its attendant 'portaloo' serve the network staff instead.

Above: The new lifting barriers, seen at Warthill on the line between York and Hull in 1952. This was the first such installation in Great Britain with flashing warning lights. British Railways, Ian Allan Library

DWG. Nº	45.LC.78.	L.N.E.R. STANDARD CONCRETE ARTICLES	CATALOGUE PAGE Nº	604
SCALE	¼"·1FT.	HUT - TYPE A	ALL LINE MATERIAL CODE Nº	661/6/40
WEIGHT	—			

Above: A typical railway hut, seen here at Marlow (GWR). In many cases the door would be on the end elevation. Ian Allan Library

Left: The LNER standard concrete permanent way hut, size A, from its 1947 concrete catalogue.

Case Study: Cromer Yard Box

The third item I built for the Cromer Project was this signalbox. It was probably the tallest signalbox on the M&GN system, and being built of timber, flexed considerably in the stiff gales that blew in off the North Sea. There was no drawing available, but fortunately there were some photographs, so I was able to make the drawing seen here to work from.

Being a timber building, I decided to construct the model from mounting board and scribe the timber frame and planking directly onto it. This meant mitring the corners so that the join would be invisible. All the window and door openings I cut out and left blank for the time being. The carcass was assembled on a small piece of plywood as the base, with an apron extending out to support the staircase, which would be added later. Lugs were added around the edge at the operating floor level, as I intended to build the operating floor as a separate entity and then drop it in. The carcass was painted in M&GN tan and buff before the next stage.

The next part of the box I tackled was the staircase. This was a real beast, being in three flights with half landings between. The only way I could see to do it was to reproduce exactly what the original builders had done, except that I would use card instead of timber. Newel posts would be small section pine, dressed off at the tops. Using the drawing as a template, I first built up the stairs themselves, with mounting card stringers and 30/thou Plastikard treads. For the landings, I fabricated beams from double thickness mounting card, again with 30/thou planking. Handrails and balustrade were cut from card, married up with the pine newel posts. Square section pine acted as the support columns, properly chamfered at the corners. Six cast iron spandrels were needed, so I drilled and cut 20/thou Plastikard into the right shape. The staircase was pre-painted before being fixed onto the signalbox.

Below: A drawing of the first Cromer Beach signalbox.

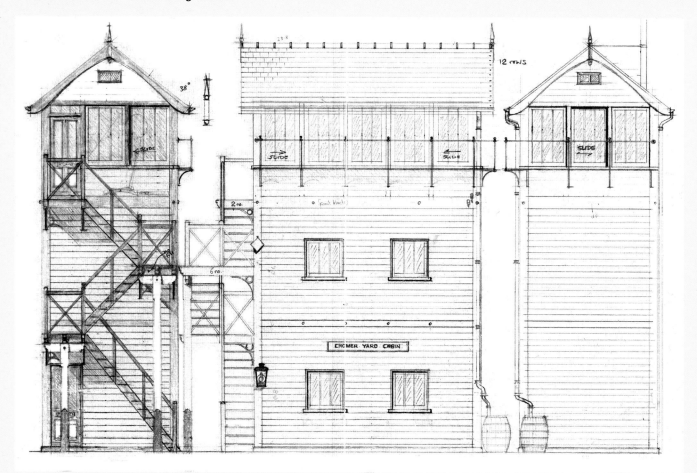

The doors and windows were made next. The doors were cut from card with the glazing added behind and a weatherstrip at the bottom. The window sashes and glazing bars were actually drawn up on 10/thou Plastikard and carefully cut out in one piece with a very sharp scalpel before being mounted on the glazing with brushed liquid solvent. The front three operating floor sashes were fixed and were made in one piece, but the others were sliding or fixed singly. There were also little toplight ventilators in each gable, and toplights over the door. These were all glued into place.

The operating floor was made as a separate unit, with its own walls, which were boarded vertically. This was the lining on the inside of the main structural frame. When the assembly was dropped into place, it also ensured that the window frames were thick where there were sliding sashes. On the floor, which I painted to resemble lino, were installed the 20-lever frame, the instrument shelf, the tablet machine and a stove. I added a noticeboard and desk at the rear, and a framed gradient diagram. I also made sure there was a signalman's duster hanging from one of the levers. Internal painting was chocolate to dado level, and cream above.

The roof was a simple card base, with added bargeboards, fascia and finials. The top was slated by the usual method of strips of thin card, although I took some trouble over the gaps between each slate, and I made one look as if it had slipped. The stovepipe has a jacket where it comes through the roof, and the lower part of this jacket slotted over the stovepipe coming up from the stove below. A flashing was added, and the wire brace, presumably installed to prevent the stovepipe being blown off.

Final details were the guttering and downpipes, the water butt (carved from dowel), the nuts for the internal bracing rods at floor level, the walkway and handrail on simple brackets, the lamp, the nameboard and the diamond-shaped telegraph fault board (which can actually be rehung to show the black fault side), and the insulators for the telegraph wires.

Above left: The imposing Cromer Beach signalbox in model form, seen from track level.

Above centre: It is clear from this angle what a complex job the staircase was.

Above right: The rear elevation and Sheringham end of the box, revealing the stovepipe and water butt.

CHAPTER

Buildings for Locomotives

6

It was realised at an early stage that locomotives would be better kept under cover when not in use. This would allow them to be cleaned and serviced mechanically without interference from the weather. To this end, the building of locomotive sheds was undertaken quite early in railway history. The building could be in a number of forms. One of the earliest was the 'roundhouse'. The concept was simple: a central turntable from which the loco roads radiated. Probably the earliest dedicated roundhouse was the original shed at Derby (1839). The external shape was circular, with the roof rising up in the centre and incorporating ventilating louvres. Other roundhouses such as Inverness on the Highland Railway and St Blazey on the Cornish Minerals Railway did not enclose the turntable and had the building arranged in a sector of a circle around it, with a door for each engine road. External walls were not always curved, but could be built with short sections of straight wall forming a polygon. The Midland and the Great Western were the only railways to multiply the use of the roundhouse, although their standard building was actually square in form.

Despite the presence of the roundhouse, the major proportion of British sheds consisted of a more simple type, which can be characterised as the 'straight' shed. This could be arranged as a through shed, which had doors at front and rear and access to both sides from the rest of the depot, or a dead-end shed, which would have access from the front only. In contrast to the roundhouse type, where there was usually one engine per road, the working of such sheds could be very complex, deciding in which order engines were to be admitted so that they did not block the way of other engines needing to exit the shed to go into traffic. There were some very large sheds to this pattern, but most engine sheds away from the major cities had four roads or less, and a great many had only a single road, which is much easier to model.

The major construction material for engine sheds was brick, although a number of sheds were built from the local stone. From the 1930s, reinforced concrete was

Below: A diagrammatic plan of a Midland 'roundhouse', this being Peterborough Midland shed, also known as Spital.

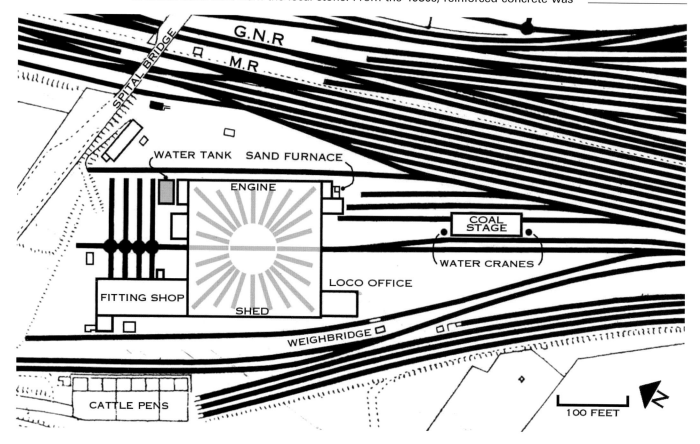

usually the chosen material. A repetitive pattern of bays incorporating large windows was a common design. The entrances for locomotives would be given large timber doors, although they were rarely closed. For roofs, the simplest choice was a gable, almost invariably in slate, although corrugated iron was used and tiles were not unknown. If the building were large, then several roofs would be arranged side by side. An alternative was the 'northlight' form of roof, a design common on industrial buildings, which featured a sawtooth profile with unequal slopes forming each ridge, and window lights on the northern side. The ridgeline was across the plan rather than along it. Along the ridges of gabled roofs would be ventilating louvres, and many smoke vents would pierce the roof, fed by smoke troughs above each engine road. This was an attempt to minimise the pollution inside the shed, which was adequate until the introduction of diesel and electric traction.

The new forms of motive power required very clean conditions for servicing, and so a programme of replacing the old steam sheds with new Traction Maintenance Depots was begun in the 1960s. TMDs resemble the standard industrial buildings seen on industrial estates up and down the country, the only difference being that they happen to be used for railway locomotives. They are often constructed using the new cladding materials, which are the modern equivalent of corrugated iron. These profiled cladding sheets are assembled on steel portal frames.

Associated with the shed would be the loco office. In here, the men would book on for duty, be given their roster details and see notices of speed restrictions or other hazards. There would also be a mess room, where crews could relax between duties. A number of sheds used old carriage bodies for this purpose until brick huts replaced them. Latrines or lavatories would of course also be needed.

Above: Ivatt '4MT' 2-6-0 No 43044 backing into the Midland roundhouse at Manningham (Bradford) in the last days of steam working. The shed, built from the local stone, has obviously seen better days and was closed in 1967. J. S. Hancock, Ian Allan Library

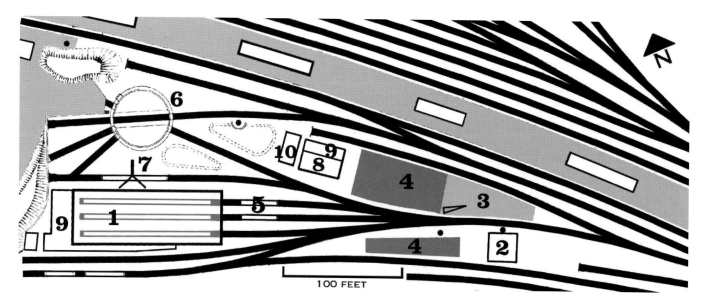

100 FEET

Above: Plan of the typical 'straight' shed at Melton Constable. Facilities are (1) engine shed and inspection pits, (2) water tank, (3) coaling stage and crane, (4) coal stacks, (5) ash pits, (6) turntable, (7) shear-legs, (8) loco office, (9) stores, (10) mess room.

The stores were a vital part of any shed, and would be the first port of call for drivers and cleaners alike. Here their oils, cotton waste and other items were stored, doled out by the storekeeper through a hatch in the wall.

Cleaning and Servicing

Until the 1940s, when wartime made standards of cleanliness impossible to maintain, it was taken for granted that most engines would be cleaned daily. To do this, a small army of cleaners was required, all of whom were on the first steps of the ladder of promotion to fireman and then driver. The cleaners would work on an engine in groups of three or four, removing the dirt and polishing the engine with tallow or Vaseline, with a 'NOT TO BE MOVED' notice placed on one of the lamp brackets. Diesel and electric locomotives, with their regular shape, are cleaned today using an automatic brush system similar to a car wash.

Cleaning also included more mundane tasks such as emptying the firebox, raking out the ashpan and cleaning out smokeboxes. All loco sheds had ash pits, and ash was shovelled from these pits into low-sided wagons shunted nearby. Mechanical systems were introduced at many sheds to make this unpleasant task a little easier.

As well as cleaning, locomotives had to be maintained in running order. Every locomotive would visit the company's works on a regular basis, where it would be disassembled and thoroughly overhauled, but many loco sheds also had considerable fitting shops where engines could be lifted, stripped down and have repairs and replacements made. The Midland standard roundhouses for example had large fitting shops attached, which could carry out heavy repairs.

As the size of the depot decreased, the facilities became more limited. All sheds had inspection pits between the rails, and at very least would have had a fitter's bench, but lifting gear was provided only at the larger ones. The smaller railways tended to keep facilities at outlying sheds to a minimum, and concentrate repairs at a central works. Highbridge on the Somerset & Dorset, and of course Melton Constable on the M&GN are just two of many.

Coaling Facilities

Originally, coaling was achieved from simple brick platforms, the coal being delivered by iron tubs lifted by hand cranes, and at many rural sheds this remained the only method. Loco coal wagons would be shunted to one side of the platform, and the labourers employed at the shed would unload them, ready for delivery to the engines' bunkers and tenders. More sophisticated methods were evolved, the next stage being a covered coal shed such as the Midland used, with one road for loco coal wagons and a central crane on a pedestal for delivery. By raising the loco coal wagon road on a steep incline, and arranging for the wagons to have bottom doors, they could deliver loco coal into hoppers, ready for easy exit via chutes to the waiting engines. In the 1920s some sheds acquired electrically operated coaling plants, where the coal would be loaded into small wagons before being hoisted up and tipped.

The final development in the 1930s was to build huge concrete coaling plants, where wagons were bodily lifted and their contents tipped into a hopper, or tipped sideways at ground level and the coal taken up to the storage hopper by conveyor belt. A chute delivered coal from the hopper into the bunkers and tenders of locomotives waiting underneath. The coaling plant at the former Carnforth Steamtown museum is still in existence, but in a poor state of repair.

Excess coal was stored in coal stacks to mitigate any supply problem. They were skilfully built up from an outer wall of brick-sized coal lumps, with loose coal within. Sometimes the outer walls were whitewashed. Every shed had at least one coal stack, but only occasionally did these coal stacks have to be used. The coal came direct from the collieries, each company having a favoured source. There were often two or three collieries used, with the coal of differing properties being mixed to the best advantage.

Loco Sand

Sand should not be forgotten. It was needed by the drivers out on the track to improve the grip between steel wheel and steel rail in slippery conditions. It was kept in small hoppers on various parts of the engine, usually under the platform, with tubes to take it to the rail and steam to deliver it to the exact spot needed. Loco sand was dried off in special sand furnaces before use, their location betrayed by short brick chimneys. The furnaces were often used for unofficial cooking purposes by the shed staff.

Below: The 'straight' shed at Basingstoke (LSWR) in 1963, with 'West Country' Class No 34054 (formerly 21C154) Lord Beaverbrook blowing off. The side walls are buttressed for strength and the front gable is glazed to admit as much light as possible. J. Scrace, Ian Allan Library

Water

Water was kept in large tanks, invariably made up from cast iron panels bolted together. There were many designs, a lot of which were specific to certain companies. The panels were typically about 4'6 × 3'6", and often had raised beading and other decoration moulded onto each panel, and even the company initials. Many tanks were built on brick bases, sometimes having swing-out arms to water the engines. The brick bases housed a pump, usually a small 'gas' engine, with the well nearby, although many companies chose to be supplied by the local town corporation. Timber piles or cast iron columns were an alternative to brick. Some engine sheds had the water tank mounted on top. A prominent feature on many water tanks was the indicator on the side, showing how full they were.

Apart from the swing-arms referred to above, there were several designs of water column, also to be seen at some stations, as well as the sheds themselves. The designs were again company-specific. The earliest were plain standpipes, where the leather bag hung unsupported. The usual format was of a long swing-arm pivoted into the main column, sometimes balanced by a large water-filled ball. The Midland's water column was like this, and easy to identify with its 'M. R. Co' cast into the top of one side. During frosty weather, braziers and tall-chimneyed stoves were trolleyed out into position and kept burning, but some columns were kept frost-free by integral gas flames.

Above: Kendal engine shed on the late David Jenkinson's 7mm layout, based on the Midland shed at St Albans, but finished in stone rather than brick. Tony Wright, courtesy British Railway Modelling

Turntables

Turntables were essential, as although locomotives could work backwards just as well as forwards, it was not ideal for the engine crew, nor was it beneficial for the equalisation of wear to the tyres. In Great Britain, the usual design was to have a pair of girders under the track, rotating in a circular pit. The ends of the girders were supported by wheels running on a rail laid around the circumference of the pit.

Turntable diameter followed the development of the steam locomotive. From an initial diameter of about 30 feet, average size increased to 50 feet by the 1890s. There things rested for some years, until replacement of older examples with 60 feet and 70 feet diameter turntables in the 1920s and 30s.

Turntables were at first all hand-operated. Many were simply pushed, in which case the perimeter of a turntable was usually fitted with raised steps to provide a good foothold. Others utilised a crank handle and gears. It was not until the 20th century that power was used to operate turntables, hydraulic, electric and vacuum methods being employed. The vacuum/air method, where the locomotive's vacuum or air brake was attached using hoses to the turntable in order to turn itself, was probably the most common.

Below: Drawing of the typical small engine shed at Cromer Beach.

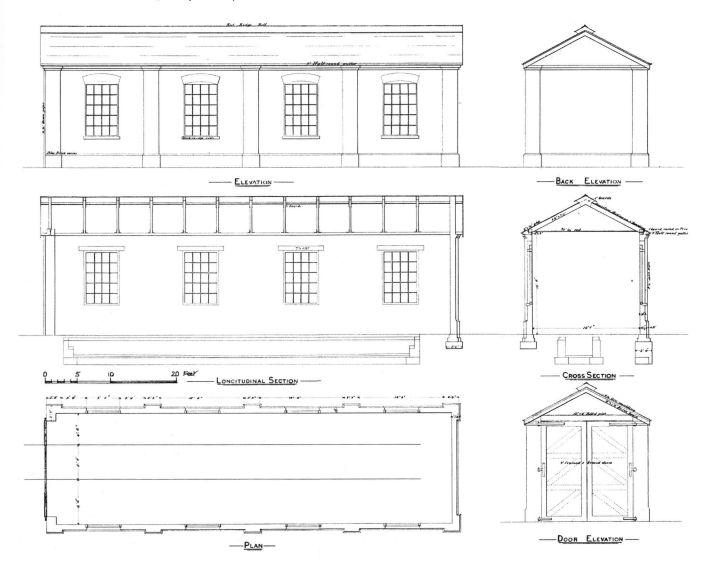

Right:. Knottingley
TMD in 1984
illustrates the
locomotive facilities
to be found on the
modern railway.
J. Rudd,
Ian Allan Library

Left: The coaling
stage at Heaton
Mersey shed, with
ex-LMS '5MT' No
44659 being watered
in 1966. This is the
second design of
Midland coaling
stage, with an
elevated wagon road.
D. S. Frith,
Ian Allan Library

Right: A typical 1930s concrete coaling tower paired with an older water tank at Dundee shed in 1966. Ivatt ex-LMS 2-6-0 No 46464 and ex-North British Railway 'J37' 0-6-0 No 64602 are being attended to.
R. E. B. Siviter, Ian Allan Library

Left: Ex-LNER Class A3 4-6-2 No 60100 Spearmint being turned by hand at Carlisle Kingmoor in 1964. The loco crew doing the pushing are half-hidden in the steam behind the tender.
A. R. Thompson, Ian Allan Library

Case Study: Cromer Beach Water Tower

The M&GN terminus at Cromer Beach had a compact running shed, which only ever had at most three or four engines allocated to it at any one time. There was a single-road engine shed, 47-foot hand-operated turntable, coal stage and water tank. I was commissioned to build the loco shed and the water tank, but so far only the tank has been constructed.

The water tank at Cromer was built on a brick base housing a small 'gas' engine, which pumped water from a borehole into the tank above. Water was delivered to the engines by a hose direct from the tank. The tank itself was made up of cast iron sections. When built, the structure was open to the sky, but in 1902 an arrangement was made with Cromer Corporation to supply town water, and the tank was roofed over to protect the regulation equipment. No drawings existed, but from photographs and the M&GN's 1:500 plans I could make the working drawing shown here.

The structure was to be made out of mounting board as usual, and as the wall area of each elevation was relatively small, I decided to emboss all the brick courses myself. This enabled me to lay out the bricks with the queen closers and not have to worry about joints between pieces of card or paper. Because the walls were panelled, and had a plinth, there were in fact several layers of card to be combined. On the reveals of the door and window openings and the recessed panels on each side elevation I continued the brick coursing by using a triangular needle file. I dressed off the bevel top to the plinth with my scalpel and made nicks for the joints between bevel bricks with the needle file.

For the brick painting on this model, I decided to experiment with a rolling method. First I made a small roller, rather like a miniature ink roller that many readers will no doubt remember from lino printing at school, by covering dowel with some leather fabric, with a galvanised wire handle. I then painted the whole structure grey, and once it was dry, rolled the brick colour on so that the mortar joints remained grey. The yellow and blue brick dressings I added by brush. All paints used were acrylics from tubes, mixed on a palette and then rolled onto the roller in just the same way as lino print ink. The result was satisfactory, but I think

Below: Drawing of the water tank at Cromer Beach.

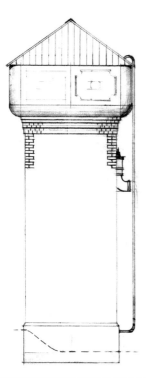
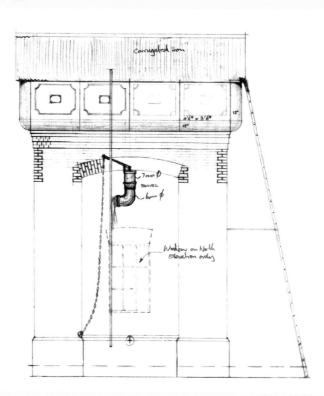
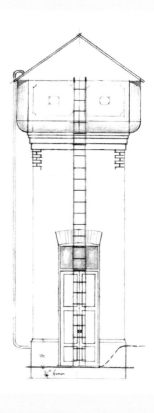

Left: The finished 7mm model of Cromer Beach tank, showing the swing-out water hose.

I may well go over the brickwork again one day with my more conventional diluted Humbrol method.

The double doors and window were made up from the usual method of cut Plastikard and card backed with glazing where required.

Having completed the brick building, I now turned my attention to the tank itself. After some thought, I decided to make this in two layers. The first was a simple box to the right dimensions, minus the thickness of the outer layer, which was to be 15/thou Plastikard. This allowed me to emboss the cast iron decoration on each panel from the rear, so that it stood proud of the surface. The inner box was simply mounting card, glued up with strips of quadrant section softwood acting as the curved corners. The Plastikard could then be bent around each corner to ensure a continuous appearance. The only problem area was at the bottom of each corner, where the shape of the cast iron panel was effectively a quarter of a dome. I infilled these areas with Das clay, and smoothed them off with 'wet and dry' paper. Painting was in the M&GN tan and buff colours.

Once the tank was fixed to the building, I added the roof, which was a simple card structure, embossed with planking in the gables (with a small hatchway in one of them) and clad on the roof surface with embossed Plastikard corrugated iron. I would have liked to use an etched ladder, but I didn't have one to hand, so I fabricated one from Plastikard and plastic rod, using a jig. To keep the ladder safe, I made a temporary base from mounting card. The building will be dropped into the baseboard when it is ready, and this temporary base discarded.

Final details were the swivel arm and water hose, chain and lever to open the water valve, and the water delivery pipe.

CHAPTER

Outside the Fence

While it is natural to concentrate on the things required to make your railway operationally complete, in order to give your railway an obvious function, the rest of the world must be represented. These are the buildings 'outside the fence' which would be of several categories such as domestic, retail, social, ecclesiastical, industrial and agricultural. All successful model railways have a believable societal structure incorporating all these categories of buildings in which to run the trains, and of course the industry and agriculture are traffic generators. The railway would have provided some of these buildings itself, as it not only built for operational function but also needed cottages and houses for its staff.

There are now a great many kits and even ready-made items for non-railway buildings, but this chapter does not give instructions on how to build these things. It is perhaps more a list of suggestions for what you should consider installing on your layout to impart a complete picture of the society served by your railway. I think the best advice I can give is simply to go out and look for yourself.

Naturally enough, the greatest number of buildings accompanying the railway would be dwellings. At the heart of almost every village or small country town would be a medieval plan. Dwellings would range from the humble cottage to the squire's Hall. Many of the buildings would have been timber framed, with upper storeys 'jettied' out. In the 18th century it became the fashion to reface these buildings in brick, and where they have not been destroyed by fire or demolished in later times, the timber frame remains hidden inside. If you are modelling modern image, then the village cottage would have been renovated and sold as a second home, and the Hall would undoubtedly be a hotel.

The way a model cottage is built and styled can inform the viewer instantly where the layout is set, but there are certain similarities. They are usually small; four rooms (two up two down) with a kitchen/scullery on the rear; their floor-to-ceiling height is often low; and the upper storey is more often than not partly in the roof, upper floor windows having dormers. The windows themselves are usually small. Roofing material varies from region to region, with differing roof pitches; thatch, plain tile, pantile and slate in decreasing order of steepness. Onto this basic pattern the differences of region and date of construction are layered.

During the Victorian period, particularly when the railway arrived, there was expansion; terraces, as seen from countless railway lines in our towns and cities, are emblematic of this period. They are useful in many ways, particularly as a

Below: The terraces of Nasmyth Street cluster tightly against Smedley Viaduct in 1971, as a DMU makes its way to Bradford from Manchester Victoria via the 'Manchester Loop'. This scene was typical of most of our cities and gives excellent modelling opportunities. M. Dunnett, Ian Allan Library

background in low-relief modelling, or as a painted backscene, plus the fact that in any one street they are usually similar or identical. Differences come in the detail – the individual changes wrought by the occupiers, such as garden sheds, pigeon lofts, or in recent times extensions or loft conversions. The railway companies themselves favoured terraces, and some of these groups of railway dwellings grew into settlements of large proportions and were provided with gas and water (and sometimes drainage) often long before neighbouring houses. Crewe and Swindon come to mind principally because there were no real settlements there before the railway. Melton Constable is another, smaller example.

The late 19th and early 20th centuries saw suburbs springing up around every city and large town for the emerging middle classes. The new suburban dwellings were heavily influenced by the 'Arts and Crafts' movement and were planned to mimic a natural village with a mix of small terraces, semi-detached and detached villas. The architecture ranges from high Victorian, to a romanticised cottage style with rustic red brick and tiled roofs. Exaggerated gables, tall chimneystacks, buttresses, and painted wooden balconies and verandahs were all very popular. The sash window that had hitherto been universal gave way to multi-pane casement windows.

Between the two World Wars, expansion assumed a slightly different form as the lower-middle classes attempted to follow their Edwardian forebears into the countryside, typified by 'Metroland', the style of building that accompanied the Metropolitan Railway out into leafy Buckinghamshire. Small semi-detached villas featured cheerful Art Deco coloured glass in their doorways and half-timbering in

Above: *The outside world beneath the railway. The extraordinary lattice girder bridge over Runswick Bay on the Keighley Model Railway Club's O gauge layout.* Tony Wright, courtesy British Railway Modelling

the gables in what John Betjeman dubbed 'Tudorbethan'. For the less affluent, detailing was simpler, but stucco or tile-hung upper storeys were still present. The terrace was a thing of the past, and it became usual to arrange dwellings in estates. This was also the time of the introduction of the council house. In urban conurbations, blocks of flats were appearing, replacing some of the worst slums, but at this stage they were low-rise, only about four or five storeys, with balcony access. It also became fashionable for the rich to have a flat in town, living in 'mansions', blocks of service flats where servants still tended to their needs. Out by the seaside, coastal towns and villages saw a rash of bungalows, some of them based on redundant railway carriages.

After the Second World War, housing stock was replenished with more semi-detached houses, council houses, bungalows, and concrete high-rise flats, which increasingly replaced terraced housing. A lot of the terraces had been razed by bombing, and much of the remainder was seen as time-expired and unsanitary and so in the 1950s and 60s a great deal of the Victorian expansion was demolished. The high-rise blocks were thought to be the answer to high-density housing, but in time they became slums themselves. At the present time they are steadily being demolished, to be replaced by standard brick two-storey dwellings and flats, ironically many in terraces. Meanwhile the surviving terraced streets are being renovated and have become desirable once again.

Traditionally, shops were mixed in with dwellings. In fact a shop would start out as simply the front room of a house or cottage being made over to retail. In the early 19th century shop fronts were expanded to display the wares in a better way, often using a bow window, where the limitations of glass-making still demanded small individual window panes. Later in the century, the manufacture of plate glass became possible and shop fronts expanded into large windows, often projecting from the front of what otherwise was still a dwelling, framed in decorative timberwork or even cast iron. Over the windows would be folding sunblinds. The modeller can have a great deal of fun depicting shop windows, such as newsagents, greengrocers or hardware shops. Mixed in with the shops are more specialist outlets such as banks, building societies, estate agents, insurance brokers, and of course today the ubiquitous fastfood chains and takeaway restaurants.

The speculative builders who drove the terraced expansion of towns and cities understood the necessity of mixing retail and domestic buildings, and every terrace had a place allocated for business at the intersection of other roads. The corner shop was born, perhaps the most typically 'British' form of retail experience. Later, during the suburban expansion it was seen as better to group shops together into a 'parade'. However, the late 19th century saw the rise of a new form of shopping: the department store. It was natural for successful businesses to expand into neighbouring properties, and every town had a large business like this, where different types of purchases were handled in departments. In the cities this was taken further, so that during the 1880s, purpose-built department stores with several floors were starting to appear. Today it is the supermarket that reigns supreme.

Public houses and inns are an opportunity to add local colour to your model. On many street corners a public house was built opposite the corner shop, and out in rural districts the coaching inn with its stables and yard still survived. Developed from the inn was the hotel, which assumed greater importance beside the railway (many city terminus buildings actually were mostly hotels) and at the seaside.

Below: The carefully observed street scene of Kendal by Arthur Whitehead for the late David Jenkinson, with a corner café and town pub. Tony Wright, courtesy British Railway Modelling

During the period before the First World War, many hotels of this kind expanded to gigantic proportions. Much lower down the scale were the boarding houses, many set up along the streets adjoining the stations, and their rear elevations with nameboards would form a background to the station yard.

Other buildings that should be included in the social mix are schools, town halls and libraries, many of which used a corporate neo-Gothic for their designs. Police stations and fire stations should not be forgotten, and over them perhaps the enormous windowless bulk of the local cinema.

When it comes to sheer size, however, a church easily dwarfs all normal buildings. There are a number of kits and models available for churches, but they all have the same fault: they are too small. One wonders how all the wedding guests frequently depicted outside a model of this kind would actually fit in. Here lies the conundrum, because if the modeller wishes to include a church and build it anywhere near the correct proportions, the model would overwhelm the layout. Some judicious reduction is obviously required. Of more manageable proportions is the chapel, standing by itself in rural districts, but often incorporated into the building line of the street in urban situations. This is particularly useful in low-relief modelling. An interesting item to model would be some ecclesiastical ruins. The landscape of England is dotted with them, where monasteries were abolished and allowed to fall down, or their materials used by the local builders. Church and chapel architecture up to the 16th century, was based largely on what we now think of as 'Gothic', but I would advise the modeller to be familiar with the ecclesiastical periods (Norman, Early English, Decorated, Perpendicular) before embarking on a church building programme. During the 17th, 18th and early 19th centuries, the favoured style was the Classical, before reverting to the Gothic during the Victorian period.

Unlike today, when what remains of British industry is usually segregated into industrial estates, industry in the past has been part of the fabric of our towns and cities. On old 1:2500 maps you will often see large buildings among the houses, marked with an industrial function. These large factory buildings were all quite similar, with regular windows on two or more floors, northlight or multiple gabled roofs, and possibly a decorative entrance and offices at the front. The nearest equivalent among railway buildings was the engine shed. There would invariably be a tall brick chimney for the engine powering the factory. Other industries had more distinctive buildings, such as the high mansard roofs and ventilators of a malthouse, a brewery, or the gasometers and retort house of the local gasworks. The tall pithead winding towers of a colliery are so iconic they need no further description. Other industrial types, such as timber yards or oil depots, will no doubt suggest themselves to the modeller. Industries of this kind were often

Below: A country inn on the Pendon Vale scene, the pinnacle of scale modelling. Tony Wright, courtesy British Railway Modelling

Above: *The church at Beeston, near Sheringham, which the author will have to model in the future. Although a very small church, it is still over 100 feet long.*

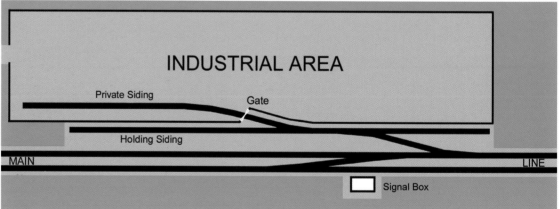

Above: *Diagram of a typical industrial private siding arrangement from a main line.*

provided with a private siding, and located in a corner next to the station can be a very effective traffic generator. Additionally, they may have been situated next to a canal or a canal basin. Canals and railways often interacted, particularly in the industrial Midlands and the North. The inclusion of a canal on a layout opens up tremendous scenic possibilities, with locks, cranes, narrowboats and barges adding interest and variety. On my 4mm 'East Walsham' layout, I have managed to include both a timber yard and a canal.

Although we tend not to think of it as such, agriculture is also an industry, particularly in the present day. Like any industry, agriculture requires buildings to service it. Farmhouses are surrounded by ancillary buildings which vary according to the type of farm. In livestock areas, these would include cow byres and milking parlours, or lambing parlours and shearing sheds. Any sizeable town in these areas would have a livestock market, which as well as being a colourful scene in itself, is another traffic generator. Cattle, sheep and pigs accounted for a high proportion of outward traffic in rural areas. Horses were another important traffic.

Arable farms would have large barns for storing produce, and nowadays grain silos. Poultry farming usually involves long ventilated sheds. In the days of horse power, a range of stables would be present, often with a pond nearby, and every village had a blacksmith. Farm machinery is stored in sheds, and with the modern day use of large harvesting machines, these sheds now resemble a standard industrial unit. Out on the farmland, there were usually a number of 'field barns' for storage away from the main farmyard. Today, most of these field barns have been sold and converted into dwellings.

Rural industries associated with farming are creameries and cheese factories, and milk in churns or tank wagons was an important traffic on the railways until quite recently. Flour mills, both water- and wind-powered, also left their mark, as did the tall conical roofs of oast houses.

Below: An example of railside industry, Oakdale Colliery in the Sirhowy Valley, South Wales, which was opened in 1908 and closed in 1989. Ian Allan Library

Above: Canals and railways often jostled for space, creating modelling opportunities. Seen here in 1967 the Leeds & Liverpool Canal is bridged by the low-level goods line to Wellington Street, and the high-level line to Leeds Central, soon to close. C. T. Gifford, Ian Allan Library

Left: Even rural industries can pack a visual punch. This is the famous Heckington windmill, one of a series with multiple sails in Lincolnshire, forming a backdrop to the ex-Great Northern station in 1988. J. Critchley, Ian Allan Library

Case Study: East Runton Windmill

The windmill is a building type, like the church, that the manufacturers have misrepresented. The only kits available are for a post mill, that is, a square wooden body, or buck, rotating on a central pivot, whereas the largest proportion of windmills in Great Britain were tower mills and smock mills. Tower mills were built in brick (or stone in the West), the diameter decreasing in a cone from bottom to top, on which a cap carrying the sails was rotated automatically to face into the wind. The smock mill was similar in form, but built of timber (usually octagonal in plan) on a brick base.

The windmill I had to build was East Runton tower mill, beside the M&GN line between Cromer and West Runton, and was the first building I constructed for the Cromer Project. Fortunately, the tower still existed and I was able to take some measurements. The cap and sails had been removed decades before, so I was going to have to do quite a bit of research to model them. The cap (without the sails) has since been restored to the tower so it now looks more like a proper windmill.

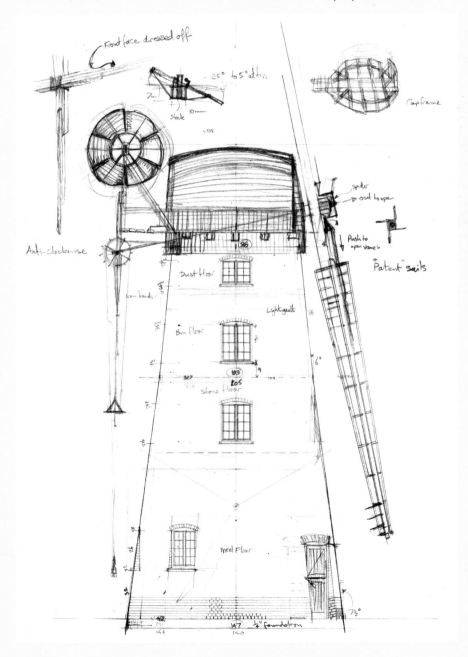

Left: *Drawing of East Runton windmill, a typical tower mill.*

Right: *Full-on view of the completed 7mm model of East Runton windmill.*

Several books have been written on the subject of windmills, so I was able to understand their construction and the names of their parts, and to track down a couple of old photographs of the original mill. In addition, I visited Stow Mill at Paston, near Mundesley, which is complete in most particulars, to make notes of small details.

The major problem with building the model was the fact that the tower was a cone; at East Runton it was actually two cones, the pitch of the slope changing about two-thirds of the way up. Commercial brick papers or embossed card would not have been able to adapt. A cone, as readers may know, can be made from a circle of card with a portion or sector removed. By using simple geometry I was able to calculate the diameter of circle needed at the top and bottom of each cone (remember there were two) and the sector of the circle needed to make the cone. I made a trammel and used it to mark out the shape on thinner card than I usually use, to enable it to bend. I also marked out the positions of doors and windows, but left them uncut for the moment.

To bend the cone, I used the same method that locomotive modellers employ to roll boilers. Placing the card shape on a folded newspaper face down, I rolled a piece of dowel over the rear, just like rolling out a piece of pastry. After a while the card was nicely curved, the process being completed by encouraging the bent card around the four floors of the mill (meal floor, stone floor, bin floor and dust floor) which I had cut out from foamcore board. Now I cut the apertures for doors and windows, but left the tower in its two parts.

The brick effect was obtained by taking cartridge paper and using the trammel to emboss the brick courses onto it. A brick tower mill is built with headers facing outward throughout. This is the only way the brick can cope with the geometry, and so I then had to scribe the perpends of each course at header spacings. It took a long time! Once I had the embossed brick paper, a piece embossed with the right geometry for each cone, I tried it on the carcass so I could establish the staggered seam at the rear, facing away from the viewing side. When ready, the brick paper was glued in place. Openings were cut in the regular way, and brick arches and cills added.

Now I had the main tower of the mill, I could turn my attention to the cap. The mill was to be motorised and so I had to house a small electric motor and a gear train to reduce the revolutions. The cap of a tower mill is built in almost the same way that a boat is built, except it is upside down. I could see no other way around it but to build the model just as the real thing was done. I added the ring, or curb, that the cap rotated on from more foamcore. The frame of the cap was built from small softwood sections, onto which I mounted the motor and gearbox I had built separately. The windshaft was of dowel fitted with a pinpoint bearing at one end, and a large gearwheel to engage with the gearbox. Where the stocks for the sails would be attached, I shaped the dowel into a square section. With the mechanism in place, I now added ribs of 40/thou Plastikard, and planked the cap with strips of 20/thou Plastikard to give the finished shape. The gallery and handrail were added around the outside, and then the fantail was built up from Plastikard and mounted on a frame of small section obechi wood. I built all this up separately, as I wanted the cap to turn on the tower.

Above: Side view of the 7mm model of East Runton windmill, showing the fantail.

Returning to the tower, I painted the brickwork in acrylics to represent the gault or yellow brick of the original, then added windows and the door from Plastikard and glazing. After access to the interior was no longer required, I was able to glue the two halves together. I then ran a tube up the centre of the tower to take the wires supplying the motor with power. The final detail on the building was to add the iron bands surrounding the brickwork at four points; at some time in the life of the mill, the owners must have been worried about the stability of the tower.

The last major item to add were the sails, or sweep. These were 'double patent' sails, made up from adjustable shutters mounted in a frame and fixed to the stocks. Adjustment was by rods cranked to a central spider, which was moved in and out by the striking rod which passed right along the axis of the windshaft to a gear at the rear of the mill, which the miller could move by means of a chain down to ground level. I made the stocks from sections of softwood, which had to be dressed off on their front faces to give the sails their angle, which turns them anticlockwise. The shutters and frames I fabricated from Plastikard.

The final detail was to add the chain and adjusting wheel at the back, and the wooden tail projecting downwards to guide the chain and to stop it swinging about. The chain is weighted at the bottom.

Bibliography

John H. Ahern, *Miniature Building Construction,* Marshall

V. R. Anderson and G. K. Fox, *Stations & Structures of the Settle & Carlisle Railway,* OPC Railprint

E. Beal, *Modelling the Old-Time Railways,* A&C Black

Gordon Biddle & O. S. Nock, *The Railway Heritage of Britain*, Studio

R. W. Brunskill, *Vernacular Architecture: An Illustrated Handbook*, Faber and Faber

W. P. Conolly, *British Railways Pre-Grouping Atlas,* Ian Allan

H. G. Forsythe, *Steam Shed Portrait,* Atlantic

D. Jenkinson, *Historical Railway Modelling,* Pendragon

David Jenkinson, *Rails in the Fells*, Peco

Barry Norman, *Landscape Modelling*, Wild Swan

Nikolaus Pevsner, *The Buildings of England*, Penguin

Chris Pilton, *Cottage Modelling for Pendon*, Wild Swan

D. Rowe, *Architectural Modelling,* Wild Swan

Signalling Study Group, *The Signal Box* , OPC Railprint

Keith Turton, *Private Owner Wagons*, Lightmoor

Trevor Yorke, *The Victorian House Explained*, Countryside Books